L I F E   W I T H

PROMISE

MARRIAGE AS A COVENANT VENTURE

Larry Martens

KINDRED PRESS
Hillsboro, Kansas
1982

LIFE WITH PROMISE: Marriage as a Covenant Venture

Unless otherwise indicated, all biblical texts used in this book are taken from the *Holy Bible: New International Version.* Copyright © 1978 by the New York International Bible Society. Used by permission of Zondervan Bible Publishers.

Library of Congress Catalog Card Number: 82-81266
International Standard Book Number: 0-937364-03-7

Cover design by Lamb Graphics and Communications
Cover photo by Don's Studio

Printed in the United States of America by the Mennonite Brethren Publishing House, Hillsboro, Kansas 67063

To Kathleen,
whose faithful and devoted love
helped me experience
life with promise

Table of contents

Introduction

A relationship is as strong as its covenant is clear.

A group is as healthy as its contract is clean.

A marriage is created by, nourished by, deepened by clear, clean covenanting.

Covenants in marriage are always multilevel.

On the conscious and verbalized level, the covenant is expressed and experienced by both partners. In some marriages, only the obvious and basic elements of covenant are put in words. All the rest is assumed by each, and the assumptions are often "recorded announcements" from the basic beliefs and values of each family of origin.

On the conscious *but not* verbalized level lie all those things each knows but is afraid to express. Thus neither knows how the other sees those beliefs or would respond to these concerns. In many marriages, this level of covenant is much larger and far more crucial than what is expressed between them. Iceberg-like, the majority lies beneath the surface, unadmitted or denied, yet directing the whole.

On the unconscious level the covenant gets more complex, confused, contradictory. Each wishes for things from the other that are unsaid since they are beneath awareness. Each hungers, longs, seeks acceptance, support, control or domination, approval or affection. Though unrecognized, this level is powerful and can profoundly form the relationship.

The more couples explore their conscious covenants and risk sharing the hidden clauses of the contract, the more these wishes, needs, fears and longings will surface and become the occasion of and content for new understanding and renewed intimacy. As we share the things we know, and express what we deeply believe, value, feel and care about, the depths of our personhood comes into awareness and enriches our self-understanding and thus our ability to understand the other.

Life With Promise offers a covenantal view of marriage which invites partners to think deeply and converse openly on the various levels of their marital promise. A covenant is a promise with length. In marriage, it is a pledge of permanence, exclusiveness, intensity and mutuality. It is also a pledge of depth — depth of feeling, depth of sharing, depth of discovery. Such a pledge commits the whole self to search for intimacy, create mutually fulfilling friendships, celebrate shared excitement, growth and joy. When a promise has length and depth, it can accept disappointment, affirm differences, appreciate the uniqueness of the other and adjust behaviorally to produce mutually satisfying relationships.

And a covenant has height; it is grounded in God who is the author of covenant-making, the creator of covenant makers, the one who is the welcoming partner to all who enter the ultimate covenant of creation and the new creation in Christ. A covenant is always more than a private promise between two; a covenant is an accountable commitment, a public pledge, a responsible vow that is made before God in the presence of community. Such a vow emerges from the solid self within a person. Its permanence is guaranteed by the person's core values, core commitments, core integrity.

Life With Promise will provide an opportunity for couples to enrich their relationship and for singles considering marriage to explore deeper meanings of living faithfully and loving unconditionally. It is a book best read jointly, discussed mutually, and assimilated into a maturing marriage. Directed at the early stages of marriage, it is useful for reading and reflecting at any of the transitions of life when a marriage needs re-negotiation and renewal.

Marriage is a gift. Two persons give to each other the privilege of intimacy with integrity. This requires work — the working through of fears of closeness and fears of abandonment. It is worth the cost of living within promises, of living out a promise.

David Augsburger
Goshen, IN 1982

Author's preface

Marriage as *Life With Promise* may seem like wishful thinking when all around us duets are turning into duels. With increasing rapidity the dreams that draw two people to the marriage altar are dashed in the human struggle of life.

In the midst of such reality *Life With Promise* suggests that the aspirations and desires of the couple at the altar can be realized. Even those marriages that have limped along for years can become growing, meaningful relationships. Based upon a covenant of faithfulness to God and to each other, marriages can be a rich venture of mutual love.

When two people covenant with each other to be husband and wife, they lay the foundation for this adventure of faith. The future is unknown, but it holds the potential for intimate, secure and joyful living. Such possibilities are not realized by accident, but through purposeful, sincere and loving commitment.

Life With Promise is a mutual life as husband and wife explore together meanings of faith, hope, love. It is a reciprocal life as husband and wife meet each other's needs in trust and caring acceptance. It is also a growing life as each person is freed to realize his or her fullest personal potential.

My hope is that this book may be a friend to all who desire growth, meaning and purpose in this interpersonal relationship called marriage. I hope young people looking forward to marriage may find inspiration in these pages. Sunday school classes may wish to use the material for a thirteen-week study. Pastors may use the book in whole or in part as grist for premarital counseling. Marriage counselors may find it useful for encounter groups. If it can encourage fellow travelers in discovering potential and hope for their marriages, its purpose will be well served.

This material was first presented as a series of studies on Christian marriage on Words of the Gospel, the radio voice of the Mennonite Brethren Church. My personal gratitude is given to Don MacNeill, executive director of Words of the Gospel, who encouraged me to put the material into book form. I am equally indebted to Jim Gaede, Dean Kliewer and George Konrad who offered their professional perspective in the preparation of the material. The force of their perceptions and understandings on Christian marriage have marked my thought and served as an inspiration in this project.

A special word of appreciation goes to Dennis Becker, who formulated the study questions at the conclusion of each chapter. It is suggested that the couple read the book together, then respond individually to the questions. Once completed, the answers should be shared and discussed. In this way the book can become the basis for communication exercises leading, we pray, toward healthier, happier marriages.

Larry Martens
January, 1982

The promise

1

Someone once suggested that fewer marriages would be on the skids if those who said "I do," did. That is a real problem. Many enter the marriage relationship knowing from the start that should problems develop, there's a way out. Couples assume that divorce is a viable option.

He: I've been giving a lot of thought to our marriage. I think it's dead. I don't have any feelings for you anymore. I've decided to file for divorce.

She: But this is so sudden. Is there another woman involved?

He: No, it's just that I don't feel anything anymore. I know we've been together for eighteen years, but the marriage is dead. We've gone round and round. I thought we could work something out, but there is no progress and I'm through. I've given up.

Divorce has become commonplace. The National Center for Health Statistics reports that there were 1,181,000 new divorces in the United States in 1979, a 4.5 percent increase over the previous year, and nearly triple the number reported twenty years ago. This means that over one million children join the ranks of youngsters under the age of eighteen who have divorced parents. If more people who said "I do," did, this great social evil could be turned around.

Taking our commitments seriously may seem a simplistic

solution, but there's nothing simple about it. Marriage is a *choice* we make. What is more, choosing to be responsible in the commitments we make is central to a secure marriage. To treat the marriage covenant casually can lead the couple down the road of unhappiness and loneliness. It often results in marital disaster.

The first marriage ceremony was performed in the Garden of Eden. God himself officiated. It is important to recall the words God used to describe that first marriage. God said, "For this reason a man will leave his father and mother and be united to his wife, and they will become one flesh" (Gen. 2:24). Husband and wife are bound together into a unique relationship! The Bible describes this relationship as a "covenant."

The Bible is a record of covenants made between God and the people of Israel. God made a pledge of faithfulness to his people, to be with them and to protect them. Israel, on the other hand, pledged to be faithful and serve no other gods. Mutual faithfulness and trust were the fabric of those covenants. The Bible uses the covenant of marriage as an analogy of this covenant relationship between God and Israel. The prophet Malachi says the Lord "is acting as the witness between you and the wife of your youth, because you have broken faith with her, though she is your partner, the wife of your marriage covenant" (Mal. 2:14).

So marriage is the result of an agreement made between two people. It is not a legal or social contract. It is a covenant. It is made under God and in the presence of fellow members of the Christian family. God himself is called as a witness to this act. God himself joins husband and wife together and "Therefore what God has joined together, let man not separate" (Mt. 19:6). Those who accept the responsibility of living together as husband and wife pledge to protect the sanctity of that marriage, and no person shall destroy that relationship.

This relationship is based on the faithfulness of the parties making the covenant. Scripture encourages us to keep the vows we make: "When you make a vow to God, do not delay in fulfilling it. He has no pleasure in fools; fulfill your vow" (Eccles. 5:4). God takes vows seriously. He remembers them as something binding. We are to keep our word. When we say "I do," we are to mean it. We are to stake our life on it. Just as God is a faithful covenant-keeping God, so we are to be faithful to the vows we make.

This covenant of marriage can be described in four ways.

The marriage covenant is a pledge of faithfulness.

If one goes into marriage saying, "I do" but means "Maybe, if things work out," or "I do, as long as love shall last," the relationship is doomed. Where there are reservations, marriage scarcely ever has a chance. This pledge of faithfulness is a promise that we will maintain the covenant of marriage no matter what. Elizabeth Achtemeier expresses it beautifully in her book *The Committed Marriage:*

> I will be with you, no matter what happens to us and between us. If you should become blind tomorrow, I will be there. If you achieve no success and attain no status in our society, I will be there. When we argue and are angry, as we inevitably will, I will work to bring us together. When we seem totally at odds and neither of us is having needs fulfilled, I will persist in trying to understand and in trying to restore our relationship. When our marriage seems utterly sterile and going nowhere at all, I will believe that it can work, and I will want it to work, and I will do my part to make it work. And when all is wonderful and we are happy, I will rejoice over our life together, and continue to strive to keep our relationship growing and strong.*

Such a commitment in marriage will endure pain, hurt, uncertainty and difficulty. People who make such a covenant do not allow events or circumstances to change their loyalties.

The marriage covenant is a pledge to exclusiveness.

When we enter this relationship we put on blinders. Our sole focus of attention is our mate. In his book, *The Art of Liv-*

---

*From *The Committed Marriage,* by Elizabeth Achtemeier. Copyright © 1976 The Westminster Press. Used by permission.

ing (English University Press, 1949) Andre Maurois describes the relationship this way: "I bind myself for life; I have chosen; from now on my aim will be, not to search for someone who may please me, but to please the one I have chosen." We vow "to forsake all others," but sometimes in our mind we add "until someone who will make me happier comes along." While the sexual revolution promotes freedom of sexual relations in and outside of marriage, Christian marriage emphasizes an exclusive relationship. The marriage covenant tolerates no rivals, and recognizes that only jealousy, hurt and bitterness can come from divided love and loyalty. Christian married love is an exclusive love.

The marriage covenant is a pledge to permanence.

Christian marriage is to last. Consciously or unconsciously, the wedding vow is often changed from "as long as we both shall live," to "as long as we both shall love." God's design is permanence in marriage. One young man asked his fiancée if she would still love him when he was bald and fat. It is probably a relevant question. But the marriage commitment is not fickle. Time may change our looks or the circumstances of our lives, but it need not change the relationship. Married love endures — and grows.

The marriage covenant is a pledge of mutual love.

If marriage is just a commitment "until death us do part," a couple might as well be cellmates. But marriage for the Christian is far more than a stark pledge of fidelity. To say "I do," and to do it, really doesn't go far enough. A union held together only because a pledge has been made cannot be called a "Christian" marriage. To be sure, the commitment provides the stability and foundation for a good marriage, but Christian marriage is meant to be more than an endurance test. It involves more than just holding something together. It is a pledge of mutual love.

This covenant relationship is not formed through negotiating a contract between two people which may make the mar-

riage more palatable for each. Rather, it is forged in love —
love of a unique character. This love focuses on giving rather
than receiving. The object of this love is not to get something
for nothing, as portrayed in many of today's TV game shows.
Rather, this love gives without expecting to receive something
in return. The uniqueness of this love is most perfectly portrayed in God's love for man. He gave his only son to die for us
without expecting us to change or to love him. His love is not
only unconditional, it never gives up on us. He never throws in
the towel. He never runs off in a huff. His relationship with us
is bathed in consistent, longsuffering love (Jn. 3:16, Rom. 5:8).

The pledge of mutual love in marriage means that we
learn to love and value one another in the same way that God
loves and values us. Christ was motivated by love even though
we were sinful, imperfect persons. He modeled a love that does
not expect superhuman faithfulness or perfection. It loves in
spite of weakness and sin.

In this sense Christian marriage is totally a relationship of
grace. The Apostle Peter even described husbands and wives as
"heirs with you of the gracious gift of life" (1 Pet. 3:7). Christian marriage is a relationship in which a person does not have
to earn or deserve love, but in which love is experienced in
mutuality. There is nothing more exciting and freeing than
to know that one may grievously err and yet be loved, accepted
and cared for.

Faithfulness in our marriage covenants brings glory to
God. That in fact is the Christian's highest goal. Paul reminds
us that we are not our own, but are bought with a price. We
are, therefore, to honor God in our bodies (1 Cor. 6:19-20). Our
ultimate goal is not personal happiness or to get our way, but
to give ourself for the happiness and fulfillment of others, of
our spouse. In doing so we fulfill our primary goal — to glorify
God.

For discussion

1. Look up "covenant" in a dictionary. In what ways is mar-

riage a covenant?

    2. When you made your marriage covenant, what did your promise mean to you? What does it mean now?

    3. Expectations are important in any relationship. What do you expect from marriage? What do you think your spouse expects from marriage? Share these expectations with your spouse.

    4. "I bind myself for life. I have chosen; from now on my aim will be, not to search for someone who may please me, but to please the one I have chosen." In what ways can you please your spouse? Ask your spouse what would please her/him.

    5. Does the Achtemeier quote express an outdated ideal? Is it workable in today's society? What will it take to make it more workable?

    6. Do you have a written or tape-recorded copy of your marriage vows? Review them together. If you don't have a copy, write a marriage vow.

Why marry?

2

You come home dog tired after ten hours of hard work on the job. Your bride of two weeks greets you with a kiss and a warm embrace. You shower and sit down to a delightful meal — your favorite: lasagne, tossed salad and cherry pie a la mode.

After supper you settle comfortably in your recliner to watch *Monday Night Football*. Two weeks of married bliss! Fantastic! It's everything you ever dreamed of! You think, "Why, that sweet little thing I married just does everything right!"

Then it comes. The voice from the kitchen. "Steve, dear, will you take out the garbage? It's in the milk carton on the table."

"Sorry, but I just got comfortable and the game's almost underway."

You hope she will catch on. After all, carrying out the garbage is woman's work. Dad wouldn't have touched it, so why should you? It isn't right for a man to start playing maid.

This time she's more insistent. "Please honey, I've got the dishes to do. It'll only take a minute."

Now you try to make your point: "Honey, I think we better make something clear from the start. There are some things men do in marriage and some things women do. I didn't get married to carry out the garbage. I bring home the bacon — that's my job. You prepare the food and keep the house clean —

that's your job."

Locking horns over garbage. It might also be drying
dishes, vacuuming the house, picking up dirty socks, folding
a load of laundry. Why do we fight and feud over such trivial
things? Generally, it happens because the marriage relationship — whether a couple has been married two weeks
or fifty years — is determined to a large extent by what we expect from each other when we marry. And many marriages are
plagued with unrealized, and perhaps unrealistic, expectations. Often what starts as a fever pitch of heavenly bliss,
grinds down to groans of agony and disgust. Many enter the
marriage relationship without ever asking, "Why am I getting
married? What do I expect from this relationship? What do
I expect to give in this marriage?" Even after the wedding
ceremony, few couples ever ask, "Why are we married?"

Unfortunately, couples spend a lot more time studying
cookbooks, financial management manuals and "how-to" books
on sex, than they do considering this relationship called marriage. Often couples spend more effort preparing for the wedding than preparing for marriage. A wedding is a highly significant event in the life of a bride and groom but it is only the
beginning of the relationship, just like birth is the beginning of
a life. A wedding is over in a single day; a marriage may last
for fifty years or more. So we should enter this relationship
thoughtfully, and understand God's purpose for it. He doesn't
leave us guessing what he had in mind for this relationship
either.

Marriage is for companionship.

It is interesting to see how pleased God was about his creation. In the creation account we find repeatedly the phrase,
"And God saw that it was good" (Gen. 1:10, 12, 18, 21, 25). God
even uses a superlative to indicate his pleasure over his creative work: "God saw all that he had made, and it was *very*
good" (Gen. 1:31, emphasis added).

The mood, however, changes in Genesis 2 where we find

the first negative: "It is *not* good." What is not good? "The Lord God said, 'It is not good for the man to be alone'" (Gen. 2:18). Aloneness was not in keeping with God's purpose and design for people. It was not what God had in mind.

This negative is part of the continuing creative work where Adam, the created man, is instructed to give names to all the creatures. But he was unable to find his own counterpart among the created beings (v. 20). So, God made a person who corresponded to Adam — physically, emotionally, socially, mentally and spiritually.

God brought the woman to Adam, and Adam responded: "This is now bone of my bones, and flesh of my flesh; she shall be called 'woman', because she was taken out of man" (v. 23). Adam recognized her as an equal. In a sense, Adam is saying, "This resembles me. I'll give her my name." And that's what Adam did. His name in the Hebrew was *Ish,* so he named his wife *Ishsha.* Some scholars suggest that by adding the Hebrew feminine ending to the word for man, Scripture intended to present woman as the weaker form of humanity. Not so. From the context it is clear that Adam is simply expressing the similarity between himself and this new creation. In a sense, Adam is saying, "What I see looks like me."

It is important to remember that Scripture is not suggesting that man and woman are totally identical beings. They are designed uniquely to complement each other. God says, "It is not good that man should be alone. I'll make him a helper suitable for him." So Adam was given a "helpmeet." She was not someone who was lower in position, but someone who was a constant source of strength and support. The word "helpmeet" is used principally in the Old Testament to describe God's help when man was not able to help himself. So this person was created to complement Adam so that she might help meet the full range of his physical, emotional, social, mental and spiritual needs. Augustine once suggested that "Eve was not taken from Adam's feet to be his slave, nor from his head to be his ruler, but from his side to be his beloved partner." This partnership is God's design for marriage.

Marriage is for sexual fulfillment.

Scripture says that man and woman are to become one flesh (Gen. 2:24). This sexual relationship was built into the very structure of creation when God made man both male and female in his image (Gen. 1:27).

We often tense up or blush when we speak of the sexual relationship. Yet Scripture celebrates sexuality as something good. The wise man Solomon saw it as something beautiful even though he couldn't understand it. He said, "There are three things that are too amazing for me, four things that I do not understand: the way of an eagle in the sky, the way of a snake on a rock, the way of a ship on the high seas and the way of a man with a maiden" (Prov. 30:18-19). Paul views the sexual relationship as a unique expression of intimacy in 1 Corinthians 7, and gives explicit guidance for both husband and wife in meeting each other's sexual needs. God created the sexual relationship to express the very pinnacle of physical intimacy and the profound depth of spiritual oneness. Far from repudiating sex as something evil, the Bible celebrates its proper use as God-created, God-ordained and God-blessed.

Marriage is for procreation.

It is God's will for husband and wife to become mom and dad. God's command to man and woman was to be fruitful and multiply, to fill the earth and subdue it (Gen. 1:28). Despite the threat of overpopulation, parenting is still a part of God's plan for marriage. The psalmist puts it graphically, "Sons are a heritage from the Lord, children a reward from him. . . .Blessed is the man whose quiver is full of them" (Ps. 127:4-5). Children satisfy a normal God-given desire for child-bearing. They bring both sorrow and joy to parents, and are often the means God uses to help parents grow to maturity as persons.

Marriage is to reflect the image of God.

Marriage is an object lesson, a picture, an illustrated sermon of God's grace and his covenant with man. What God had in mind more than anything else when he ordained marriage was to establish a covenant between man and woman so that this relationship could be a constant reminder of God's love for humanity.

Paul had this in mind when he described marriage in Ephesians 5 as a reflection of the relationship Christ has with the church. It is pictured as a relationship of subjection and sacrificial love. Christian marriage is to be like a billboard advertising the quality of God's love for women and men.

A young woman once suggested that she was looking for a good Christian man so she could have a Christian marriage. She no doubt became painfully disappointed as she entered marriage. Too often we think a mate is supposed to do for us what only God can do. Many find it difficult to be married and also to be Christian because they try to fill their spiritual God-shaped void with a spouse. It won't work. God created us for himself, and our hearts will be restless for him even in marriage. We must love God first, and experience the power and fulness of his Spirit in our lives. It is through him that we are able to find happiness and fulfillment in life with our mate.

We do what we do because of what we are. Only God's love and forgiveness can heal what we are. When our hearts have been filled by the love of the Christ, our minds gripped by the good news of the gospel, and our nature filled by the Holy Spirit, we are able to experience the meaning and fulfillment God designed for Christian marriage.

For discussion

1. In addition to the four purposes listed in this chapter, are there other purposes which you can identify? What led you to choose to be married? Might you choose to be married for different reasons now?

2. Think carefully. In what ways are males and females different? How do these differences make them suitable for companionship?

3. Why might a married couple desire to have children? Why might they choose not to have children?

4. "Christian marriage is to be like a billboard advertising the quality of God's love for people." What do marriages which you observe say about God's love? If you are married, what does your marriage say about God's love?

5. What roles do you expect to fulfill in marriage? What roles do you expect your spouse to fulfill? Did you and your spouse answer these questions the same way? Will you need to make adjustments?

6. Expectations are important in any relationship. What do you expect from your marriage? Why?

Cutting the
apron strings

3

A couple came for counsel. He was almost sixty years old. She, his fiancée, was in her mid-fifties. They wanted to marry, but faced a special problem. His mother, who was almost ninety years old, would not give her blessing to the marriage without a special recommendation from a marriage counselor. And he refused to marry without his mother's blessing. This was the man's third marriage. It too ended in failure because he was unable, even at his mature age, to free himself from his mother's influence.

When should a couple break parental ties? Is it ever possible to make a clean break? Furthermore, when two people join in marriage and establish their own home, whose life-pattern do they follow in this new home? The pattern she learned in her family, or the pattern he learned in his?

The Bible has some good advice: "For this reason a man will *leave* his father and mother and be united with his wife, and they will become one flesh" (Gen. 2:24). Children are to "leave" their fathers and mothers. The word "leave" means to break free, become detached or released from something. For the married couple it involves "cutting the apron strings."

Making clean breaks

Unfortunately, many never make a clean break. Couples may leave home physically, but remain tied to their parents psychologically. If no real leaving takes place, the marriage will be in trouble.

Mother-in-law jokes reflect the difficulty children have in breaking ties with their parents, or the difficulty parents experience in releasing their grip on their children. When a marriage takes place, the attachment to home and parents must be replaced with an attachment to one's mate. This does not mean disregarding or dishonoring one's parents. Rather, it means that the ties to one's parents are severed so the couple is free to form this new relationship.

Breaking free from the parental influence does not mean that the family of origin is unimportant. Strong family ties should be continued, but the new couple must be free to form their own pattern of life together.

It is not the paternal parents' marriage; it is not the maternal parents' marriage; it is to be uniquely the new couple's marriage. Under the direction of the Holy Spirit this new creation can be shaped and designed with a personality all its own. Just as a newborn baby cannot grow up unless the umbilical cord is severed, so a marriage is unable to grow as long as there is no real leaving or clear separation from parental influence.

Breaking ties isn't easy

Severing the parental relationship is a two-way street. It involves decisive action by both parents and children. The parental role in this process is probably the most difficult. Children are often more anxious to leave than mothers and fathers are to let them go. Parents have so much invested in their children. They brought them into the world, nurtured them to maturity, and invested much energy, love and concern in their lives. But parents need to loosen the apron strings and allow their children freedom to carve out their own lives.

Parents must relinquish their "first" claim upon their children. The parental home will no longer be their home. Parents will no longer be responsible to look after their physical, material, emotional and spiritual needs. Now a new relationship is formed. It is a new home. While they remain the children of their mother and father, they have now moved to a new status as equals to their parents. They too are husband and wife, fellow adults, hammering out this new married relationship. They may not be as experienced as their parents, but they need freedom to grow, mature and even struggle as they give shape to this new relationship.

Contracting the break

Ideally, releasing children for marriage should be verbalized in some form by the parents. Writing out their feelings and sharing them with the bride and groom prior to the wedding may be helpful. Sometimes the wedding ceremony itself includes a statement from both sets of parents expressing their support and encouragement for the marriage. The statement may include something like the following:

> These children belong to us. We brought them into the world and nurtured them. Now we relinquish our first claim upon them; we give them to each other. Our homes will no longer be their homes, but their home will be the new one, which is the fulfillment of our love and prayers. Henceforth our discipline of them is ended; we are no longer responsible for their character and conduct; they are in each other's care and guidance; we will not deal with them as children but as fellow adults whom we greatly love.*

To agree publicly to release parental authority and to entrust children to their new home is a helpful way to encourage the firm bonding of the new marriage covenant.

Walter Trobisch suggests in his book *I Married You* (Harper and Row, 1971) that parents can be compared with chicken hens that hatch duck eggs. "After they are hatched, the ducklings walk to the pond and swim away. But the hens cannot follow them. They stay on the banks of the pond and cackle." We parents may be concerned, but we no longer have control over them. To free our children is to give them space to grow and mature in this new relationship of marriage.

Children also have an important function in this leaving

---

*From *In Holy Marriage*, by George Sweazey. Copyright © in 1966 by Harper and Row, Publishers, Inc. Used by permission.

process. Leaving doesn't mean that children abandon, ignore or mistreat their parents. Leaving means cutting the emotional, dependent strings that once provided security, protection, financial assistance and physical care. If children bring these ties into the marriage, it will hinder the sealing of the marriage bond.

Severing parental ties can result in a kind of grieving process. Often parents are fearful whether their children will succeed. Sometimes they may question the choice of spouse their children made. They may vividly recall their own struggle with marital adjustments, and wonder if the children will be able to survive on their own. Children can make the break with parents less painful by assuring their parents of their love, by maintaining open lines of communication, by inviting their parents to dinner, and generally fostering a warm and cordial spirit in the relationship.

This leaving process can also be verbalized by the children. One couple, while still on their honeymoon, wrote their parents a letter that went something like this: "Mr. and Mrs. Sam Brown want you to know that we are the happiest couple." After thanking the parents for a gift they had given, the bride continued:

> "Folks, you are just *great*. . . Sam and I want to thank you for putting on such a lovely wedding for us. There is not one thing we would want to change. We think that we had a perfect wedding. . . . Last night when we got to our room we had devotions. While Sam was reading in Psalms the tears began to roll down my cheeks. I had all kinds of mixed feelings. I was so happy to be Mrs. Sam Brown; we have waited so long for this, and yet it was so sad to leave my dear family. Sam was so good and patient with me. He will be a great husband."*

What a beautiful way of helping parents break the ties.

Leaving mother and father requires a high level of maturity for both parents and children. Parents will need to resist

---

*From "Loosing the Apron Strings," an unpublished sermon by Marvin Hein, (n.d.). Used by permission.

the temptation to continue the parental roles. They must free their children to assume the new adult roles of husband and wife. On the other hand, children will need to focus their attention on the new relationship that is being created. They will need to resist the temptation to run back to mother and father for encouragement, comfort or affection. Such needs are now to be met through their spouse. The couple's first priority is to each other and their new home.

Severing parental ties takes time and involves significant personal adjustments for both parents and the newlyweds. Change is never easy — a new relationship like marriage is no exception. Cutting the apron strings involves risk and may at times be painful, but it opens the door to new growth and potential. "For this reason a man will leave his father and mother." It is God's design for Christian marriage.

For discussion

1. Reflect upon your own home. Do you or your spouse still have some uncut parental apron strings? What makes you aware of them? Are some positive? Negative? How are you dealing with them?

2. Write a letter to your parents thanking them for their care during your growing up years. Tell them about your marriage.

3. How would you describe your feelings when you left home to start a new marriage? How did your parents feel? Was there any grieving?

4. How do you view your parents' marriage covenant? How does it influence you? Would you like to emulate that commitment? If not, what would you like to do differently?

5. Reflect on the following statement: "While they are still children, they have moved to a new status as equals to their parents." Is this too idealistic? Are children ever equals with their parents?

6. How can you prepare yourself to free your children to leave home? How can you prepare your children to leave home?

Marital freedom — life with limits

4

Many people marry for better or for worse, but not for good. They view the relationship as temporary — easy in, easy out. Short-term commitments are the name of the game. The courts are even simplifying the matter with "no-fault" divorce. It is getting cheaper too. I recently saw a billboard advertisement which read, "Divorces — Cheap, $45." A hit song by Paul Simon of the recent past describes the process of breaking off relationships painlessly:

> The problem is all inside your head she said to me;
> The answer is easy if you take it logically,
> I'd like to help you in your struggle to be free,
> There must be fifty ways to leave your lover.
>
> You just skip out the back, Jack,
> Make a new plan, Stan,
> You don't need to be coy, Roy,
> Just get yourself free.
> Hop on the bus, Gus,
> You don't need to discuss much.
> Just drop off the key, Lee,
> And get yourself free.*

While such a casual, free-and-easy spirit permeates our thinking today about marriage, these attitudes stand in stark

---

*© 1975 by Paul Simon. Used by permission.

contrast to the words of Jesus, who reaffirms the validity of the Genesis 2 claim: "For this reason a man will leave his father and mother and *be united* to his wife, and the two will become one flesh. So they are no longer two but one. Therefore what God has joined together, let man not separate" (Mt. 19:5-6).

But isn't a lifelong marriage relationship obsolete? Isn't marriage "until death us do part" a thing of the past? Some suggest that as life patterns have changed, so marriage too must change. Some specialists in marriage and family recommend an "apprentice period" for people contemplating marriage. Such marriages would have a five-year termination clause with the option of renewing or canceling the contract.

How does this sound: "I, Jim, take you, Sue, to be my lawfully wedded wife for the next five years." This alternate arrangement is sometimes referred to as serial monogamy and offers individuals the right to change partners from time to time. Such freedom would become a fully recognized, socially acceptable and inherent right of marriage partners rather than a reluctant concession.

Others recommend a voluntary open-ended association between man and woman which frees marriage from legal ties. In this case, the vow would go, "I, Jim, take you, Sue, to be my wife as long as it is mutually agreeable." Voluntary association would provide the freedom to exchange partners without guilt or the painful snarls of legal hassles should the relationship not work out.

Are such flexible, easily altered commitments the answer for those who cry for greater freedom in man-woman relationships? Does marriage mean the end of personal freedom as some suggest? Is commitment in marriage the loss of voluntary, spontaneous love? Just the opposite is true. Commitment in marriage is the basis of true freedom!

The freedom of a lifelong relationship.

Many could give witness to just the opposite. A lifelong covenant in marriage does not violate the personal freedom of marriage partners. True freedom comes, paradoxically, not in freedom from limits, but in a lifelong commitment. Limiting one's freedom can actually be freeing. The boundaries of an athletic field limit the freedom of the players while at the same time freeing them to play with abandon. Only if there is agreement about the limits is there any freedom in the game.

God has set the boundaries for marriage. It is a relationship with limits. The limits, like glue, bind the relationship: "A man will leave his father and mother and *be united* to his wife" (Gen. 2:24). To these words our Lord added, "Therefore what God has joined together, let man not separate" (Mt. 19:6). This relationship binds man and woman together as husband and wife. They stick together because they have committed themselves to each other. The relationship now limits their freedom while also freeing them to enjoy each other fully, freely, securely.

Such lifelong commitment finds its model in the relationship God had with Israel. God is in fact portrayed in Scripture as the husband of Israel who has established an eternal covenant with his people (Jer. 31:32). No matter how wayward Israel might be, God is faithful to that covenant.

One of the beautiful portraits of this covenant relationship comes to us from the experience of the prophet Hosea. Hosea married a prostitute by the name of Gomer. In spite of the marriage covenant, and even though children were born to Hosea and Gomer, she left her family and continued her life as a prostitute. What should Hosea do? Should he end the marriage? God counseled Hosea to cling to his wife, and love her in spite of her shameful and despicable life.

A beautiful scene unfolds in the narrative. Gomer is auctioned off as a prostitute. Hosea scrapes together some money and buys her back. He says to her, "You are to live with me . . . you must not be a prostitute or be intimate with any man, and I will live with you" (Hos. 3:3). Here is the model for the marriage covenant: longsuffering love, compassion, faithfulness (Hos. 2:19-20).

The freedom of a loving relationship.

Marriage is not based on emotional, passionate love. We have been sold the great lie in our day that the essence of marriage is love. To be sure, love is an important ingredient in the marriage relationship, but love is an emotion. It may be strong today and gone tomorrow. Love also may be selfish, or nothing more than fickle admiration. "Love," as David Augsburger suggests in his book, *Cherishable: Love and Marriage* (Herald Press, 1971) "is only love when it offers itself in total fidelity, unafraid of the future." In other words, love flows out of one's *commitment* to a person. It is not the *basis* of that commitment.

The freedom of an exclusive relationship.

True marital freedom comes from the security of knowing that there is only one lover. Rivals in a marriage relationship create confusion, hurt, uncertainty, alienation. Infidelity binds, rather than frees, and violates the warm and tender trust that comes from an exclusive love. A relationship of faithfulness liberates the spirit of husband and wife for a creative, enjoyable freedom with each other.

This freedom is also rooted in the thought life of the marriage partners. Our Lord said that to lust for someone in one's heart is as much adultery as the act itself (Mt. 5:27-28). Our Lord knew that unfaithfulness can bind a person in secret mental infidelity. So he challenged us to safeguard our marriage covenants by refusing to allow the imagination to dwell on such thoughts that would violate our own or another's fidelity in marriage.

The freedom of a primary relationship.

The primary relationship in a family is husband and wife, not mother and father. God did not start with a parent and a child in the garden; he started with a husband and wife. And the instructions he gave for that relationship describe marital, not parental functions.

Unfortunately, our society has shifted the priority from the husband-wife relationship to the parent-child relationship.

The result is deteriorating marriages. It is no accident that the greatest number of divorces occur during two periods of major adjustment: the first three years of marriage and after twenty years when children leave home. Too many parents feel guilty that they are neglecting their children if they take a weekend away just for themselves. If marriages are to grow, parents need the freedom to focus on the primary relationship, their marriage, without overlooking their secondary concern, the children.

Our society needs to cultivate an attitude that the marriage covenant is a binding, permanent relationship. Such an attitude toward marriage is good for us psychologically. All of us need the security that we will be loved, cared for and understood even when we are weak or when we fail. Our children need the atmosphere of a stable, secure, loving environment which is conducive to healthy and vigorous growth. Finally, our own full spiritual development as husband and wife requires an atmosphere where love, joy, peace and faithfulness abound. Such a life is possible in a relationship with the one who said, "So if the Son sets you free, you will be free indeed" (Jn. 8:36). In him we are bound; in him we are free!

For discussion

1. *What do you think is the most important ingredient in keeping a marriage together?*

2. *With all the broken marriages around us, what is it that has kept you and your spouse together?*

3. *How does a lifelong covenant provide freedom in marriage?*

4. *Of the freedoms listed in this chapter — lifelong relationships, loving relationships, exclusive relationships, primary relationships — which do you need to work on? What will you do to live in that freedom?*

5. *How do the media — television, magazines, movies — portray marriage? Is there real freedom in these portrayals?*

6. *Since children demand so much of parents, how might*

couples maintain their two-person relationship despite their duties with children?

7. Write a letter to your spouse, expressing your desire to give freedom in a particular area. Share your letter and then discuss it together.

The honeymoon
that never ends

5

The musical *Fiddler on the Roof* is the story of Tevye, a milkman, and his wife Golde. After twenty-five years of marriage they finally talk about their love relationship. We hear the following dialogue between them:

Tevye: Golde, I'm asking you a question. Do you love me?
Golde: You're a fool.
Tevye: I know. But do you love me?
Golde: Do I love you? For twenty-five years I've washed your clothes, cooked your meals, cleaned your house, given you children, milked the cow. After twenty-five years, why talk about love right now?
Tevye: Golde, the first time I met you was on our wedding day. I was scared.
Golde: I was shy.
Tevye: I was nervous.
Golde: So was I.
Tevye: But my father and my mother said we'd learn to love each other. And now I'm asking, Golde, do you love me?
Golde: I'm your wife.
Tevye: I know. But do you love me?
Golde: Do I love him? For twenty-five years I've lived with him, fought with him, starved with him. Twenty-five years my bed is his. If that's not love, what is?
Tevye: Then you love me?
Golde: I suppose I do.
Tevye: And I suppose I love you, too.

Tevye and Golde: It doesn't change a thing, but even so, after twenty-five years, it's nice to know.*

Love! How is it expressed in your marriage? Is it verbalized? Acted out? Or, is there death-like silence when you talk about the more intimate aspects of your marriage? While love in its varied forms is a normal part of the man/woman relationship, people like Tevye and Golde just never talk about it.

In addition, we often carry into marriage certain myths which prevent us from realizing the full range of marital joy and fulfillment. One such myth suggests that man and woman are radically different in their response to the love relationship. Women are more concerned with the emotional atmosphere of the relationship while men focus on the physical side of marriage. This myth suggests that it is not natural for men to be tender or in need of care and security. One person shared another myth with me when he said bluntly, "Women don't have any sexual feelings."

Indeed, both men and women were created sexual beings. Their maleness and femaleness were created by God to complement the other's emotional and physical needs. Furthermore, it is entirely proper to express one's "maleness" or "femaleness." But to suggest that only women can have tender feelings, or that only men have sexual drives is to misrepresent God's creative work.

Scripture says, "At the beginning the Creator 'made them male and female' . . . and the two will become one flesh. So they are no longer two, but one" (Mt. 19:4-6). Our Lord affirms a reciprocal relationship where the emotional and physical needs of both husband and wife are met. "One flesh" describes a unique, creative level of mutual intimacy that expresses the highest and deepest love humanly possible.

The sexual relationship evokes a variety of responses

*From *Fiddler on the Roof* by Joseph Stein. Copyright © 1964 by Joseph Stein. Used by permission of Crown Publishers, Inc.

today. Some people think of it as something good; others evil. Some think of it as enjoyable; others merely tolerate it. Some respond to it out of desire; others out of a sense of duty. Some see it as the ultimate expression of love; others selfishly practice it for physical release. Some complain about not "getting enough"; others are accused of being a "cold fish." Clearly, both church and society need positive guidance on the issue.

Scripture offers no fully developed, systematic teaching on the sexual relationship. The following are some biblical principles which offer help in shaping our attitudes on this important issue in marriage.

God created the sexual relationship as something good.

Male and female beings were designed by God to meet one another's physical needs (Gen. 1:27-28; 2:24-25), and what he created he called "very good" (Gen. 1:31). Psychologist and author Henry Brandt says, "God has not made the human body with good parts and bad parts; he has made it all good." The sexual relationship can be evil if it is perverted, but there is nothing in the Bible that supports the idea that what was designed by God for the married relationship is evil. Rather, biblical writers revel in the goodness of God's creation, and marvel at the unique creative handiwork of God.

Sexual sharing is only for the husband and wife relationship.

Throughout Scripture God makes it clear that the sexual relationship is to be enjoyed only by married partners. In our world of wife-swapping, swinging and unisex this may sound prudish. People who enjoy affairs outside their marriage may view fidelity in marriage as out of touch with the times. Some believe that there is nothing wrong with a little "extra-curricular" activity.

Or is there? Is free love ever totally free? Isn't there always a price to pay? It may offer momentary joy, but it often leads to emptiness, despair and grief. One woman involved in an extra-marital affair described it as both a "blessing" and a "curse." The reason? Free love is sexual activity without the commitment of the whole self. To be "one flesh" with a person is nothing less than the involvement of the whole person in that relationship. Paul suggests that to be involved in an adulterous relationship is to pervert one's soul because he "sins against his own body" (1 Cor. 6:16-19). Paul is arguing that sexual sharing without the full commitment of self is to pervert one's spirit by misusing one's body. When we do that we violate the intention God has for the relationship between man and woman.

Sexual sharing without love and commitment is a mirage. Helmut Thielicke, a German theologian, suggests in *The Ethics of Sex* (Harper and Row, 1964) that the sexual character of a human relationship involves the rhythm of attraction and repulsion, passion and indifference. We alternate between hurting and healing, estrangement and reconciliation. Romantic passion comes and goes. It rises and falls. Fulfillment turns to apathy. These momentary states of ecstasy disappear like a vapor. That is why people involved in adulterous relationships become disillusioned, unhappy, angry and bitter. Blessing does become a curse. It is only sexual sharing based on a covenant of trust, fidelity and commitment that can offer an ongoing, meaningful and fulfilling experience.

God designed the sexual relationship for pleasure.
Our Victorian attitudes reflect the notion that anything pleasurable is evil. Not so in God's design for marital intimacy. The sexual act provides marriage partners with exhilarating and pleasurable delights. God intended the sexual act to be the ultimate expression of married joy.

Furthermore, this relationship is designed to meet the needs of both husband *and* wife. Paul says, "The husband should fulfill his marital duty to his wife, and likewise the wife to her husband. The wife's body does not belong to her alone but also to her husband. In the same way, the husband's body does not belong to him alone but also to his wife" (1 Cor. 7:3-4).

Clearly, Paul is referring to unselfishness in the sexual

act. Both husband and wife have the pleasure and delight to fulfill the sexual desires of the other. Sex isn't a selfish drive. If it's healthy, it's unselfish. That's God's design for the physical joys of marriage. What a significant difference it makes when both husband and wife realize that the sexual relationship is not simply for their own satisfaction.

The sexual communication expresses a unique love.

True love is not just an emotion. Erich Fromm suggests in *The Art of Loving* (Harper and Row, 1956) that "To love somebody is not just a strong feeling — it is a decision, it is a judgment, it is a promise." True love is action on behalf of another.

Theologian Victor Hugo once wrote that "the supreme happiness in life is the conviction that we are loved." Most of the world would agree, but not our Lord. We learn from him that "It is more blessed to give than to receive" (Acts 20:35). For him love was more than an emotion; it was a decision. He offered himself for our benefit without expecting anything in return.

To be sure, to *be* loved is important. It reassures us of our value, respect and dignity. It removes doubts about our self-worth. It frees us from the pain of insecurity. Best of all, to *be* loved is to feel accepted in spite of our inadequacies, our weaknesses, our faults. The greater gift, however, is *to* love. The deepest form of love concentrates on giving, and the most significant gift we can give our spouse is ourself. Give freely, spontaneously, joyfully! Dwight Small suggests in his book, *After You've Said "I Do"*(Revell, 1976) that two married people rich in love for each other can say, "Now abideth romance, sex and love — these three, but the greatest of these is love."

This love of which I speak is slow to lose patience — it looks for a way of being constructive. It is not possessive: it is neither anxious to impress nor does it cherish inflated ideas of its own importance.

Love has good manners and does not pursue selfish advantage. It is not touchy. It does not keep account of evil or gloat over the wickedness of other people. On the contrary, it is glad with all good men when truth prevails.

Love knows no limit to its endurance, no end to its trust,

no fading of its hope; it can outlast anything. It is, in fact, the one thing that still stands when all else has fallen. (1 Cor. 13:4-7, *Phillips*)*

For discussion

1. *Of the four principles of the sexual relationship mentioned in this chapter, which creates the greatest tension for you? Why?*

2. *Respond to the question, "Is free love ever totally free?" Why? Why not?*

3. *In a sentence or two, give your reason for staying with the biblical injunction for sexual sharing only in the husband/wife relationship.*

4. *How is love expressed in your marriage?*

5. *What do you like most about your sexual relationship? What do you like least?*

6. *From your childhood experiences and training, how do you view sexual relationships? Good? Bad? Tolerable? Enjoyable?*

7. *How do male and female complement each other in sexual relationships?*

---

*Reprinted with permission of Macmillan Publishing Co., Inc., from *The New Testament in Modern English, Revised Edition*, J. B. Phillips, translator. © J. B. Phillips 1958, 1960, 1972.

The intimate affair

6

He comes home from work, this time only *one* hour late. He looks in the kettle. "Hmm, stew again? Smells burnt." She simmers, "You don't miss a day do you? You gripe about my cooking every day and twice on Sunday." He retorts defensively, "Aw, cut it out. I make an occasional suggestion, maybe, but I give you your share of compliments too." She cuts him off with, "Yeah, sure! Yesterday you complimented me on the steak — called it 'fried sole of shoe,' wasn't it?"

Marital bliss? Hardly! It's more like living next to a volcano which threatens to explode for the umpteenth time.

Intimacy, warmth, openness, love, affirmation, grace, forgiveness, acceptance, caring, joy — that's the way we'd like it to be. Put-downs, coldness, disappointment, hurt, bitterness, anxiety, fear, uncertainty, misunderstanding, rivalries, jealousies — that's more the way it is.

Is it possible to work through differences in tastes, ideas, habits, attitudes and patterns of living? Are husbands and wives able to share dreams, hopes and fears in a relationship of openness and intimacy? I believe so, but it doesn't come easy. It takes much energy, a lifetime of commitment, and a deep-seated dedication to one's marriage partner.

Marriages are made up of people with differing needs and ways of relating. Some find intimacy exciting, others find it threatening. Many erect all kinds of barriers to in-depth rela-

tional experiences. David Augsburger describes seven personality types who represent negative styles of relating and differing barriers to intimacy.*

Nellie Nagger: Nellie is shrewd and critical, and never
forgets faults in others.

Gert Gunnysacker: Gert collects grievances and refuses to
deal with problems as they arise, brooding over them until she
reaches the bursting point.

Burt Battler: Burt is irritable and defensive and fights
back when exposed or pressed.

Orville Overkill: Orville annihilates all the opposition by
overreacting to circumstances. He drops the A-bomb when a
hand grenade would do.

Willie Withdrawn: Willie would rather flee than fight. He
is a true dove who takes long walks or goes for drives rather than
face confrontation.

Vivian Vesuvius: Vivian seems even-tempered and good-
natured until she gets angry. Then everyone gets a blast: husband, kids, the entire neighborhood.

Annie Analyst: Annie is a first class secret agent. She
must have everything explored and explained, and constantly
judges the motives and intentions of people.

Marriage brings together such variety in people: the imperfect, fearful, uncertain, defensive, finite. They are, never-
theless, individuals with potential for significant, in-depth
levels of intimacy.

Intimacy is not something that originated with psychologists or even marriage counselors. It was part of the design
when God created man and woman to be husband and wife.
Scripture outlines four progressive steps toward marital intimacy: "For this reason a man will leave his father and mother
and be united to his wife, and they will become one flesh. The

---

*From *Cherishable: Love and Marriage,* by David Augsburger. Copyright ©
1971 by Herald Press. Used by permission.

man and his wife were both naked, and they felt no shame" (Gen. 2:24-25).

Leave — cleave — one flesh — unashamed! These progressive steps are a developmental process that involves breaking parental ties, being bound together in faithfulness to this new relationship, uniting physically as man and woman, and developing an open and transparent relationship between man and woman. This fourth level, hammered out according to God's design, offers married partners a unique, meaningful, open, confident, trustful, fulfilling and enjoyable relationship.

What does the Bible mean when it says, "The man and his wife were both naked, and they felt no shame"? It reflects an interpersonal transparency. They had nothing to hide — no hidden agendas, no hangups, no embarrassment, no fears. And, in that relationship this first married couple experienced unrestrained freedom — emotional as well as physical, inward as well as outward.

It is interesting to see what happens to this couple in the next chapter of the Genesis story. Adam and Eve are living in a perfect environment, experiencing what we today would describe as a perfect relationship. God is walking in the garden looking for them. He calls to Adam, "Where are you?" Adam replies, "I heard you in the garden, and I was afraid because I was naked; so I hid" (Gen. 3:9-10).

Why the coverup? Adam and Eve had sinned. Because of sin, they became self-conscious. It never dawned on them before that they were naked. Charles Swindoll says in his book, *Strike the Original Match* (Multnomah Press, 1980), "Their unguarded transparency prompted unrestrained intimacy with each other." The original design is beautiful, attractive, open, transparent. It is free, confident, trustful, fulfilling, enjoyable. But sin brought guilt; guilt resulted in shame; shame caused them to hide. Sin divides and erects walls between people, obstructing free and open communication. Sin causes intimate relationships to become a frustrating struggle — a strange

mixture of selfishness, embarrassment, dissatisfaction and re-
sentment. God's design is a relationship of unrestrained intimacy.

How can one move to greater levels of intimacy in marriage when the walls are up and we feel more like strangers
than intimate friends? It doesn't happen with a simple "I do" at
the marriage altar. Rather, it is a lifelong growth process of
two individuals who cultivate a unique climate where intimacy
can be nurtured.

Several principles can guide the marriage partners in that
growth.

Intimacy grows best when we risk openness.

Intimacy grows when we are willing to become vulnerable
with each other. We sometimes believe that ignorance is bliss.
In some situations that may be true, but not in marriage. To be
intimate involves the risks "to know" and "to be known" by our
marriage partner. The Old Testament term for this kind of intimacy means "to know." The term implies sexual intercourse
— Adam "knew" his wife Eve and she gave birth to a child
(Gen. 4:1). But it also means much more than merely physical
union. For Adam to "know" his wife meant the union of Adam
and Eve in body, mind and spirit. It involved the rational, emotional and spiritual dimensions of the human personality. "To
be known" adds another dimension to intimacy. It involves the
sharing of oneself — to risk one's thoughts, aspirations, desires
in an atmosphere of openness and trust.

For those who refuse to be open and candid, and instead
close themselves off from one another, we must say, "no openness, no intimacy." Intimacy is not available to those who cover
the problems of the relationship with saccharine-sweet conversation. Intimacy will never grow if we pass off the painful
realities with a shrug, or hide the warts and wrinkles by pull-
ing the blinds to our real selves.

Intimacy grows best when we tune-in to each other.

The wife says to her husband who is hiding behind the

newspaper, "I feel like you're a thousand miles away." Present but absent. There is little joining or linking of thoughts and feelings in such a relationship. The couple isn't really "present." One person confesses, "I feel so alone when I'm with you." The "we" or "us" feeling never develops. Marriage is "stillborn" unless husband and wife tune-in to each other and learn to interact on significant levels by sharing feelings, dreams, fears, uncertainties and hopes.

Intimacy grows best when we care about each other.

"How did work go today?" can be more than just a meaningless conversation filler for people who care. People who care are sensitive to the moods, attitudes and feelings of people. This caring goes beyond the routine needs of health and physical well-being. It also says, "I care about what you think and what you feel." Caring also moves to the unresolved conflicts which tend to force us apart. It refuses to ignore such tensions as though they don't exist. People who care recognize that unresolved conflict can eventually destroy the relationship.

Intimacy grows best in a climate of trust.

Some people desire privacy and find open, free, spontaneous conversation difficult. Others like to share everything and expect others to reciprocate. True intimacy respects the needs of each individual and makes no demands. Trust respects the need to be alone, or to be partially open. Trust means *voluntary* openness, where the relationship is free and communication unforced. Lois Wyse puts it well as she describes this principle at work in her marriage:

> There is within each of us
> A private place
> For thinking private thoughts
> And dreaming private dreams.
>
> But in the shared experience of marriage,
> Some people cannot stand the private partner.
>
> How fortunate for me
> That you have let me grow,

> Think my private thoughts,
> Dream my private dreams.
>
> And bring a private me
> To the shared experience of marriage.*

There is a natural human rhythm of needing to be together, but also to be alone. A growing relationship recognizes such needs and accepts them comfortably.

Deeper levels of marital intimacy are not achieved overnight. Rather, the growth of intimacy is a lifelong process of two persons who are committed to work at it. In some ways intimacy is like a skill which must be learned and cultivated through disciplined practice. Yet intimacy cannot be hammered out through sheer effort, power or manipulation. Intimacy grows best in an environment of mutual care and trust.

Scripture describes husbands and wives as "fellow-heirs of the grace of life." This relationship of grace enables us to live and grow in a spirit of harmony, sympathy, love, compassion, humility and peace (1 Pet. 3:7-11). Such interpersonal qualities provide the atmosphere essential for the growth in intimacy.

Aesop's fable "The Wind and the Sun" illustrates the principle. The wind and the sun were arguing over who could get the coat off the man. The wind said, "I can blow the coat off." He began to blow. But the harder he blew the tighter the man held the coat around him. Finally the wind gave up. The sun then began to shine quietly on the man until he became so hot he took the coat off voluntarily. Intimacy and closeness will not be achieved with wind techniques. Grace and love help husband and wife warm up to each other making possible deeper levels of intimacy.

For discussion

1. Of the seven personality types described by Augsburger, which comes closest to describing you? Your spouse? Does your

---

*From *Love Poems for the Very Married,* by Lois Wyse. Copyright © 1976 by Garret Press.

spouse agree with your perception of yourself? Do you agree with your spouse's perception of himself/herself?

2. Do you find it easier to share freely with people other than your spouse? Why? Why not?

3. Think about the four climates for the growth of intimacy — risking openness, tuning in, caring, trusting. Which climate do you need to develop? How can you develop that climate in your marriage?

4. What sort of things might you imagine you could never share with your spouse? What kinds of things might you wish to share with your spouse in the future?

5. What kind of "wind techniques" have you used to get your spouse to open up?

At least friends

7

"I want to be treated like a precious gem." These words, spoken by Carolyn Schuller to her father Robert Schuller, aptly describe the kind of treatment many newlyweds want from each other. They want someone who sees them as special, worth caring for, valuable, precious. Do I treat my wife like I would treat an expensive diamond or a gold watch? Is she my friend? Do I treat my husband as something to be valued? Cherished? Is he my friend? Shouldn't husbands and wives be "at least friends"?

After listening to a couple describe their marriage problems and the pressures of child-rearing, I asked them, "When was the last time you went out together, and did something just for you?" The husband scratched his head: "I can't remember." The wife chimed in, "It's been a long time."

Like many couples, friendship was once an important part of their relationship. Now it had all but disappeared, displaced with other things like parenting, jobs, bowling leagues, PTA and church functions. These activities are good in themselves. There is nothing anti-marriage about having children, working or being involved in recreational, civic or church activities. Yet such concerns often compete for marital friendship. Functions have their set times; there is a structure, perhaps even a deadline. Friendship has none of this. It is often just "squeezed in." As a result, it usually gets "squeezed out." Two people who

37

once enjoyed a meaningful friendship often become more like strangers.

Our Lord has some important things to say about friendship: "Greater love has no one than this, that one lay down his life for his friends. You are my friends, if you do what I command. I no longer call you servants, because a servant does not know his master's business. Instead, I have called you friends, for everything that I learned from my Father I have made known to you" (Jn. 15:12-15).

It seems clear that our Lord thought of love and friendship as linked together. Friendship is not motivated by a set of laws, but by love — a new dynamic for life. This love is to be the inner source of motivation for all human relationships.

True friendship can be characterized in five ways.

True friends make time for each other.

Strong friendships require time and special attention. A lick and a promise will never do. Our Lord chose to spend time with his disciples. Other things were secondary to that relationship. He was not satisfied with just "squeezing in" a little time here and there.

True friends do not allow jobs, time schedules, family or community events to destroy the relationship. True friends make time for each other because they are comfortable together and enjoy each other's company. Friends like each other and want to share time together.

True friends respect each other.

"I no longer call you servants . . . . Instead, I have called you friends." Masters give orders and servants follow them without questioning their purpose or meaning. Friends, on the other hand, are concerned with the dignity and value of personhood. Domination of one person over another will never do. Respect is needed if friendship is to develop.

This respect doesn't whittle away at the other, or put the other down. Put-downs are demeaning and attack personhood.

Friends treat each other with respect and cherish each other as persons.

True friends serve each other.

"Greater love has no one than this, that one lay down his life for his friends." Friends expect good things from each other. But they don't wait for the other person to move. They take the initiative even though it may be risky. They may get turned down, but that's all right. Friends know that when they are turned down it is for a good reason, or at least without malice.

Because friends look out for each other, the relationship is not easily shaken. It can survive anger and conflict, and is secure in the face of turmoil. Friends do not cover their anger with forced silence or a false grin. They let each other know when they are displeased. They know the relationship can take it because they have learned to trust each other with their deep feelings.

This friendship is not just a "fair-weather" relationship. Friends don't turn away from each other if things go wrong. Since marriage is based on an eternal covenant of love, external changes do not affect the character of the relationship. These friends are concerned less with personal gains or losses, and more with how their marriage partner is doing. True friends in fact give up personal gains for the happiness of the other.

True friends share with each other.

"I have called you friends, for everything that I learned from my Father I have made known to you." Married couples with healthy friendships keep no important information to themselves. They are open with those things which affect the relationship. They listen carefully to each other. They hear what the other person says and they listen for the feeling messages too.

People who are both married and friends also give and receive from each other. They love to invite the other to go for walks or drives, to have a bite to eat, to take in a concert, to visit mutual friends and even to run errands for each other. They enjoy making the other happy.

Of course, a husband and wife were never meant to be all things to each other. We can expect too much of friendship. We should not try to make that one relationship the entirety of our existence. We need room to be apart from even our closest companion. At the same time we must be sure that our friendship doesn't slip out the back door because of our preoccupation with our own agenda. True married friends have at the top of their list concern for their spouse.

Friendship in marriage springs from a deep and deliberate commitment to each other as husband and wife. Married friends make a promise, or covenant, of mutual care and support on their wedding day, but their relationship is a continual reaffirmation of that covenant with each other. They do not choose to be friends only during courtship and engagement. They renew their covenant of friendship with each other again and again.

When questions arise about the relationship, such a couple takes the time to call each other back to the basic agreement. They both feel the pull of that covenant. Furthermore, they are not slow in monitoring the temperature of the relationship to see if there are symptoms of a potential difficulty. When there are problems they take measures to insure that healing can begin. This is the kind of friendship that is crucial to good marriages.

Are you friends with your marriage partner? If not, why not sit down together and take your friendship pulse? What do you need to do to put friendship back into your marriage? Make specific plans; project specific activities. Your plans may be very simple, like taking a walk, riding bicycles, playing a game. Or it may be a weekend for just the two of you, free from children, work and schedules — freedom to enjoy each other, to renew your friendship as husband and wife. Our Lord's friendship with his disciples is a good model for us. Let's not sacrifice to other demands the time and energy we owe our marriages.

For discussion

1. Read again the pages giving the characteristics of true friends. On a scale of one to five, one being the highest, rank yourself and your spouse on each characteristic. Have your spouse do the same. Compare and discuss the results.

2. Think of ways that you can treat your spouse like a "precious gem." What can you do just for each other?

3. What activity or attitude might be getting in the way of your relationship with your spouse?

4. Think of persons in your past who exemplify a model friendship in a marriage relationship. What kind of friendship characteristics do you admire in them?

5. Discuss the statement: "A husband and wife were never meant to be all things to each other." Do you agree? Disagree? Why?

One plus one
equals three

8

A woman once told me that she had never had a disagreement with her husband in over thirty years of marriage. I have often reflected on her comment. Like many, she believed that the essence of a happy marriage is the absence of conflict. She thought that to be one in the marriage covenant meant always to agree.

In contrast, another couple, reflecting on the many differences of opinion they had had in fourteen years of marital battles, observed, "We figure that if we always thought and acted alike, one of us would be unnecessary."

Shouldn't true lovers have similar tastes, interests, dreams, likes, dislikes? Isn't that what Scripture means when it says that "two shall become one flesh"? Unity in marriage means *sameness*, doesn't it?

Not really. That is, in fact, another myth of marriage. Many people enter marriage believing that differences in thinking, feeling and acting are a threat to true marital love. Indeed, such differences at times can be dangerous and destructive. But diversity can also be desirable, even necessary. For man and wife to deepen their marital intimacy, the two must share their differences.

It is God's design for marriage: "So God created man in his own image, in the image of God he created him; male and female he created them" (Gen. 1:27). Husband and wife were created male and female and were formed as unique beings patterned after God's own image.

Unity not uniformity

In Hebrew the words of Genesis describe these persons as "man-he" and "man-she" — two parts of one unity. Genesis 2 enlarges the image by describing man and woman as complementary beings who provide those qualities lacking in the other. Man and woman are not to be carbon copies of each other. They are creations with personal qualities and characteristics which make them unique individuals.

This creates an interesting paradox in married love: two beings become one, yet remain unique persons. They do not, nor should they, lose their personal identity. David Augsburger says it well in *Cherishable: Love and Marriage:* "The two-ness must not be engulfed by the one-ness." Every marriage must find a balance between unity and individual freedom. A unified couple has common goals and purposes, but allows — even encourages — the development of individual interests and abilities.

Psychologists tell us that it is impossible to experience real unity in marriage unless both people enjoy a separate identity. Only when you feel sure of yourself as a unique person can you give yourself completely to another. When we are sure of our own identity, we are able to move to greater depths of intimacy in relationships with others.

Charlie W. Shedd, in his book *Letters to Phillip*, describes marriage as the forming of a river by the convergence of two streams. At first, each stream flows along independent of the other, smoothly and quietly. But as they converge, they clash and hurl themselves at each other in a display of tremendous energy. Then the water flows on as a river and quiets down, developing a quality all its own, now broader, more majestic and much more powerful.

In the same manner the marriage covenant is formed with the convergence of two lives. The husband brings his total being with its parental influences, personality, needs, goals, hopes, dreams, drives, tastes, ways of thinking, feeling, loving. The wife brings her total being with its different versions of the same basic ingredients. The old systems, however, are not obliterated as they form the new system called marriage. They converge with each other, life with life, in a creative force to shape a new existence as husband and wife. *The two become three.* The man's life system and the woman's life system join to form the married life system. Each person retains his or her uniqueness, but gives totally to this new relationship as husband and wife.

Oneness, not sameness

Much of the struggle in marriage has to do with the tensions created by the relationship of these three systems. It is in fact the struggle of the "me" with the "we." The husband's "me" and the wife's "me" are often like two poles that repel each other. As these two "me's" come together there is a clashing of the wills, ideas, goals, aspirations, religious beliefs, patterns of thought, lifestyles. We often think of this struggle as something negative or undesirable, something to be avoided. It can, however, become a creative force to stimulate the development of significant marital intimacy. Ultimately, the goal of marriage is to achieve a sense of the *we* without demolishing the *you* or the *me*, says Wyden George Bach in *The Intimate Enemy* (Avon Books, 1968).

Unfortunately, much of our experience is, like one person described it, an adventure comparable to going off to war. Another couple said, "If, during our stormy matrimonial voyage, we do come to occasional patches of calm sea, we cannot enjoy them; we are too seasick from the other experiences."

When Kathleen and I were married we brought our individual "me's" to our marriage relationship. Like most marriages, ours has had its ups and downs. We have often struggled in allowing both "me's" to be active. We have found the relationship to be at times painful and unproductive. Early in our marriage Kathleen, in total frustration, once went home to her parents. She was ready to abandon the relationship. Her parents wisely took no sides, and sent her back to work on the problem. In our growth as persons, we have begun to discover rich meaning and fulfillment in marital intimacy. We are learning (after twenty-three years) that *oneness* in marriage does not have to be *sameness*; *unity* does not mean *uniformity*. We are learning that diversity can be an asset, not a liability.

This is the pattern God established for his church. Scripture describes the church as a unified body formed by Christ's Spirit (Rom. 12; 1 Cor. 12; Eph. 4). Yet, there is diversity in that body. Each member contributes his or her unique gift for the benefit of the whole. And each gifted person is necessary to bring the body to full maturity in Christ. This principle is also true in Christian marriage. Each partner contributes to the growth of the other and to the overall maturity of the marriage.

Our need for space

In order for this to happen husbands and wives need to be careful that the "me-ness" is not engulfed by the "we-ness." "I can't stand to be separated from you," may sound good in a fairy tale, but it doesn't work well in real married life. Eventually someone begins to feel smothered. We need to allow space in our togetherness. Kahlil Gibran put it well:

> But let there be space in your togetherness
> And let the winds of heaven dance between you.
> Sing and dance together and be joyous
> But let each one of you be alone.
> Even as the strings of a lute are alone
> They ought to quiver with the same music,
> And stand together, yet not too near together.
> For the pillars of the temple stand apart,
> And the oak and the cypress grow not in each other's shadow.*

---

*Reprinted from *The Prophet*, by Kahlil Gibran, by permission of Alfred A. Knopf, Inc. Copyright 1923 by Kahlil Gibran and renewed 1951 by Administrators C.T.A. of Kahlil Gibran Estate, and Mary G. Gibran.

Unfortunately, our society tends to think of marriage as one-sided. We tend to view man's role as primary, woman's as secondary. Men are free to be individuals, growing to their fullest potential. Women, however, often are expected to function as nothing more than an extension of their husband. In some instances they are no more than another important piece of property, along with the house, automobile, boat, swimming pool or business. In many marriages the wife is like an employee who runs errands for hubby, or she must play the role of a smashing sex symbol who must leave a good impression on the boss or a business prospect. The wife's personality can easily become trampled under such expectations. Her interests and abilities are stifled, and she may feel exploited and something less than a full person.

The Lord's great commandment to "love our neighbor as we love ourselves" is instructive. Neighbor love means to have equal regard for each other. That means that I love my wife and her uniqueness as a person to the same degree that I love myself. She is to love me and my uniqueness in the same way that she loves herself. This concern for equal regard should supersede our concern for headship and authority, or position and roles in the home. Our value as marriage partners does not come from what we do. Our value comes from our personhood. We are cherishable people. Each possesses equal value. Each contributes significantly to the growth and development of the marriage.

While we are one in marital purpose, we are unique individuals. Margaret J. Hess writes in *Eternity* magazine, "We owe it to a partner not to rob him of the capacity to function as an individual" (March, 1977). To treat each other with equal regard is helping both partners reach full potential as marriage partners. And that leads to stronger and more mature marriages.

For discussion

1. If you are single, think of the kind of person who would complement your personality, talents, characteristics. If you are married, how do the personalities, talents and characteristics of you and your spouse complement each other?

2. Where do you and your spouse experience tension as you come together to form a third unit?

3. Define "oneness" and "sameness" in marriage. How do we develop "oneness" without "sameness" in a marriage relationship? Identify areas in your marriage where you and your spouse share "oneness" but not "sameness."

4. Think about the following statement: "Conflict can stimulate growth and maturation of persons and strengthen the marriage relationship." Under what circumstances would this happen? Are those circumstances present in your relationship?

To know,
to be known

9

A marriage relationship is only as good as its system of communication. This system of communication is the means by which husband and wife learn to know each other. As we said in Chapter 7, the covenant of marriage is like an agreement we make with each other *to know* and *to be known*. *To know* my spouse means that I am able to understand what she thinks, feels, values, loves, fears, desires, hopes. *To be known* means that my spouse understands what I think, feel, value, love, fear, desire, hope. Communication is the dynamic interchange of ideas and feelings that makes that process happen.

Communication between husband and wife is a topsy-turvy world. Take Joe for example. He tells the guys at the plant what a good cook his wife is. He brags how unusually tasty her dishes are. The food they serve in the plant cafeteria is garbage compared to the meals she prepares, he boasts.

Joe goes home after work, looks through the mail and notices an unusually high phone bill. He seethes inside when he counts the number of long distance calls to his in-laws. Then Joe and his wife sit down to supper. The fare? Liver and onions. Joe blows his stack. "What kind of cook are you? This stuff would disgrace a garbage heap!"

What happened? Joe praised his wife's cooking to the boys, but now he rips it to shreds at the supper table. Liver and onions may not be Joe's favorite dish, but it's quite obvious that

Joe's anger is not over food. He's angry about the phone bill. But Joe has a problem letting his wife know what he feels. Instead of talking about the real issue, the phone bill, he attacks his wife's cooking.

The process of communication involves sending messages (encoding), and receiving messages (decoding). Some of the messages we send (encode) deal with ideas and information. We refer to it as verbal communication. Some of the information we share is given with gestures, smiles, frowns, shrugs, tone of voice, or posture. This nonverbal communication can carry feeling messages of care and acceptance, or anger and rejection.

Communication also involves receiving (decoding) the messages. We receive a message when we hear, see, feel and comprehend the message. Many times the real messages are not sent clearly. Joe sidestepped his real concern about a high phone bill when he sent his wife the message, "You're a lousy cook."

Sometimes the message is never accurately decoded. A couple was walking in the park enjoying its beauty. The lush, green scenery was enhanced by the singing of a choir in a nearby church and the chirping of crickets. The girl said, admiring the choir's effort, "Isn't that beautiful music?" The fellow replied, "Yes, and I understand they make it by rubbing their hind legs together."

To communicate effectively both the one sending the message and the one receiving the message must work at accurately encoding and decoding the message. The one sending the message must carefully frame the information both verbally and nonverbally so the desired message is clearly communicated. The one receiving the message must work at understanding both the verbal and nonverbal information in order to accurately understand the message sent.

Good communication has as its central purpose to make clear everything that partners expect of each other. It is concerned with keeping current all issues that affect the relationship. Communication is that process which allows two people *to know* each other and *to be known*.

Paul, in writing to the Ephesians, describes how the walk of the believer involves clear communication. He mentions four qualities which strengthen the communication system.

Communication must have integrity.

Paul says, "Therefore each of you must put off falsehood and speak truthfully to his neighbor, for we are all members of one body" (Eph. 4:25). In this chapter, Paul discusses the uniqueness of the Christian's walk in the world. He stresses that sound relationships are impossible apart from integrity in our communication with one another. Since we are united in spiritual unity, honesty and openness should characterize our exchange. So he says, "speak truthfully to your neighbor."

Speaking truthfully means being honest with one's feelings. For Joe that means talking about the phone bill, rather than attacking his wife's cooking. Speaking truthfully means saying what we really mean and feel.

Likewise, speaking truthfully assumes honesty. We must reflect our feelings accurately. Speaking truthfully means that we refuse to disguise our anger with saccharine-sweet words. We refuse to hide our true feelings even though expressing them may be risky.

Speaking truthfully also involves speaking for self and not for others. It is saying, "This is what *I* think and feel" instead of "People think. . ." or "You get the feeling around here. . . ." It also refuses to put words in the mouths of others, "You don't really mean that, you mean. . . ."

Moreover, speaking truthfully involves the receiver of the message. At times the "decoder" may need to ask for clarification or additional information in order to understand the message clearly. In doing so, however, one should seek to avoid questions that come across as put-downs. "What do you mean by that?" can be interpreted as "Will you tell me your meaning again?" or "How dare you say that to me!"

Communication should be emotionally controlled.

Paul says, " 'In your anger do not sin.' Do not let the sun go down while you are still angry, and do not give the devil a foothold" (Eph. 4:26-27). Communication can be thoughtful, gentle, gracious, loving. It can also be bitter, hateful, destructive, hurtful. Paul acknowledges the valid expression of deep emotions like anger. But we need to be careful not to vent anger with lethal, below-the-belt attacks. The Bible urges the management of anger. Anger can be managed when we express it in appropriate ways — by dealing with the cause of the pain we feel, or correcting the behavior that has disrupted the relationship.

Anger that is managed appropriately does *not* ignore the issues that generate the anger. Harbored resentments can destroy a relationship. So we need to pursue the resolution of anger each day. Paul says, "Do not let the sun go down while you are still angry." Keep the issues current. Avoid the notion that the problem, or even the anger, will go away. One person has suggested, "When I repress my emotions my stomach keeps score." Repressed or ignored anger hurts and keeps hurting. Anger will disappear only when we take the appropriate action to flush out the bitterness and hostilities from the relationship through confession and forgiveness.

Communication cherishes people.

Communication needs to be person-minded. Paul reminds the Ephesians that positive attitudes toward the person takes priority in our conversation. The *person* is always more important than the *problem* and the *relationship* is more important than the *words* we express. *What* we say is important, but *how* we say it is infinitely more important. Are our words armed with daggers? Or are they bathed in grace? Paul says, "Do not let any unwholesome talk come out of our mouths, but only what is helpful for building others up according to their needs, that it may benefit those who listen. . . . Get rid of all bitterness, rage and anger, brawling and slander, along with every form of malice. Be kind and compassionate to one another" (Eph. 4:29-32).

On one level, Paul refers here to language that is foul, putrid and rotten. Such language, of course, is always out of place in the conversation of Christians. But "unwholesome" words can also include words that are unfit or degrading. So Paul encourages us to avoid conversation that tears down by systematically dicing and cubing a person with sarcastic or inflammatory comments. We hear them often: "How dumb can you get?" "Boy, aren't you the high and mighty."

Instead, Paul reminds us to pour our energies into speech that builds and values the other person. We are to speak with a gracious, kind, tender heart of understanding and care. This kind of speech is less concerned with setting the record straight than it is with the feelings of our mate. This conversation cherishes each other.

Good communication is maintained through confession and forgiveness.

Our communication system can short out, or be filled with static because of the attitudes we often bring to the relationship: lack of acceptance, fear, disappointment, anger. So Paul has some helpful advice: "Be kind to one another, forgiving each other, just as in Christ God forgave you" (Eph. 4:31-32).

Breaks in the communication system can be cleared up through confession and forgiveness. If we are bitter, blow our stack, make a big scene, attack with put-downs, or carry around grudges, we need to confess such sins and ask for forgiveness. Confession and forgiveness help clear the channels for strong, positive signals of gracious communication.

We're often like misguided automobiles. We collide and dent each other's fenders; we smash each other's headlights; we bang each other's rear ends. It's important that we practice the dynamics of reconciliation in our marriages. We dare not ignore even scratched fenders.

Good communication between husband and wife requires a covenant that is sound enough to risk *knowing* one's mate fully, and secure enough *to be known* without risking judgment or rejection. Such a communication system is the lifeline of a good marriage.

For discussion

1. Read again the section on qualities which strengthen communication, pp. 50-52. Notice the specific suggestions. Choose one suggestion for each of the four qualities to practice this week.

2. When it comes right down to it, how well do you think your spouse knows you? How can you tell if your spouse is really open and honest with you?

3. Is your communication system on a collision course? What will it take to put it back on a safe course?

4. One way of communicating is with "I messages." "I feel ___ when you ___ because ___." This helps us to clearly express our feelings without making other people angry. Is there something — positive or negative — which you would like to tell your spouse? Put it into an "I message." Then tell him/her.

5. What are your life-goals for the next five years in the following areas: vocation, family, marriage, spiritual life and recreation? If you are married, share your goals with your spouse. If you are single, tell another significant person.

For better,
for worse,
or for more?

10

In *Strike the Original Match*, Charles Swindoll tells the story of a young girl who heard the story of Snow White for the first time. She was totally taken up by the story and was anxious to share it with her mother. When she got to the climax she said, "And Mommy, do you know what happened then?" Her mother replied, "I suppose they lived happily ever after." "No they didn't," the girl retorted, "they got married." The little girl seemed to sense what many married people soon discover — marriage and unhappiness are not mutually exclusive.

Many people today believe that good marriages are free from conflict. On the contrary, conflict is an inevitable and inescapable part of a relationship where two people seek to live in close and intimate levels.

Differences are normal

The conflicts are quick to emerge. The covenant of marriage brings together two people with differing family backgrounds, styles of home life, interests, intellectual abilities, gifts or talents and emotional states. These differences make us special, unique persons yet they are also the grist out of which disagreements, conflicts and crises arise.

Crises in marriage often begin in innocent ways. The following example, admittedly exaggerated, illustrates the tragic tendencies.

54

He (to friends): On our way over here a green Mustang cut in front of us and just about forced us off the road!

She: It wasn't green, it was blue.

He: It was *green*. I saw it! *(Implying he has better eyesight.)*

She: It was blue and you know it! *(Implying that he never admits he is wrong. Already it is more than a simple disagreement. There are insinuations of weakness and the two begin to fight over a pointless issue.)*

He: It was a 1979 green Mustang. You weren't even paying attention to what was going on. You were feeding the baby.

She: I saw precisely what happened. It was blue and you know it. You're color blind.

He: Get serious. You were turned the other direction, and it happened so fast — you couldn't have gotten a good look at it. Besides, you wouldn't know the difference between a car and a truck anyway.

She: I resent that!

He: Resent it all you want! It's the truth! That's the problem with you — you can never admit you might be wrong! You're just like your mother!

The disagreement has now turned into a vicious "I win, you lose" battle. Furthermore, the focus has switched from the color of the car to personal attacks, with both husband and wife fighting a personal battle for control and power.

The Book of James has some important things to say about such interpersonal struggles. "What causes fights and quarrels among you? Don't they come from your desires that battle within you? You want something but don't get it. You kill and covet, but you cannot have what you want. You quarrel and fight" (Jas. 4:1-2). James not only describes the attitudes which precipitate such fighting, but observes, "You want something you cannot have." We want to win, but a good fight is never a "win/lose" affair. Defeat or victory is never experienced by only one person in a marriage conflict. The nature of the covenant is that either both win, or both lose. And fear of losing causes us to use lethal weapons in the conflict. Such fighting becomes vicious and hurtful. The goal in marriage is togetherness, understanding, reconciliation and deepening intimacy. So the goal in resolving conflict is not a technical knockout, but a caring, loving embrace.

Conflict can be positive

People experience a variety of feelings from the word "conflict." Some associate the word negatively with destruction, violence, disorder. Others view the word positively and think of conflict as adventure, opportunity, excitement, development, or even fun. Some correlate conflict with competition, rivalry or bargaining. Most people, however, think of conflict as an evil that will destroy the relationship. True, conflict can destroy. But conflict can also spur growth and maturation of persons, and thereby strengthen the marriage relationship.

It is interesting that conflict always crops up within relationships that matter. If the relationship didn't really matter, the conflict would not have arisen. That's why in the covenant of marriage, conflict can be viewed as something to be expected. That also helps explain why we are often afraid of conflict. We are fearful that conflict may destroy the relationship.

It doesn't need to. Working through conflict can lead to deeper levels of marital intimacy. The marriage covenant provides the foundation for the resolution of conflict. When husbands and wives cherish each other as persons and hold dear the relationship they have as husband and wife, the foundation is laid to work through interpersonal conflicts. But finding solutions for marital conflicts requires that couples move beyond their fears and negative notions and search for positive, constructive ways in dealing with conflict.

Dealing with conflict

People deal with interpersonal conflict in a variety of ways. One may use one or more of the following approaches.

Some are negative; some are positive.

Withdrawal. A couple came for counsel. They were married for twelve years, then divorced. Now they wished to restore their broken marriage. They had a classic love-hate relationship, but never displayed their hate with big outbursts of anger or conflict. The wife dealt with conflict by clamming up. The husband withdrew into a book or magazine or took a drive in the car. The husband even found his extended business trips a means of withdrawal. Silence may be golden at times, but it can also be yellow. Withdrawal is never an acceptable manner with which to deal with conflict.

Smoothing over. We may say to ourselves: "Oh, it's no big deal. He'll get over his anger. He'll change." We may even piously feel like a suffering servant for the sake of marital peace. Smoothing over may be a technique we use to ignore the malignancy that has infected the relationship.

Force. At times we may resort to force, manipulation or our position of authority to resolve conflict.

He: I'm the head of this household and the wife is to be subject to her husband.

She: You're right. I am to submit to you. Forgive me for being so headstrong.

That may sound spiritual, but it isn't. Instead of dealing with differences, the issues are buried under the weight of intimidation. Force — whether physical, verbal or spiritual — often causes our conflicts to erupt later in undesirable, destructive ways.

Compromise. Here each party bargains with the other.

He: I'll go to the museum with you tomorrow, if you will go fishing with me today.

She: But, I went fishing with you last week, too.

They work out a compromise. Bill will go to the museum on Sunday and the concert on Tuesday if Sue will go fishing with him today. Each party gets part of what they want. Compromise is a part of every healthy relationship, but should never be a screen to avoid the differences which still exist. The truce can only be temporary.

Confrontation in love. The goal in resolving conflicts in marriage is to find solutions that are productive and satisfying for both husband and wife. The goal is not for one to win and the other to lose, but for both to win. But how? The only acceptable solution is to handle the differences by confronting the problems openly and honestly in mutual love.

Some forms of confrontation can be brutal, painful, destructive. The effective model of settling differences, however, brings together two elements: love and truth. Love and truth are like the positive and negative poles on a battery. Both are essential if the car is to start or the lights to burn. Love and truth are essential if husband and wife are to work through their differences to the satisfaction of both. In *Caring Enough to Confront* (Regal Books, 1981), David Augsburger describes these two elements as the arms of genuine relationship: confrontation with, and affirmation with love. Augsburger refers to this style of communication as "carefronting."

This way of dealing with interpersonal differences says, "I care about you. I care about our relationship. I care about your viewpoints. I respect your feelings. I value your insights." But it also says, "I care about me. I want you to understand my viewpoints, my feelings, my insights."

Confronting in love refuses to withdraw, smooth over, ignore, or even settle for compromise. It knows that the real issues are settled when both husband and wife express their differences openly, candidly, lovingly and caringly. We make our desires clear: "I feel deeply about this issue." "I want to express clearly what I feel." "I want your clear, honest viewpoint." "I want your caring response."

At times, we use each of the above methods of dealing with differences. A brief survey of the life of Jesus reveals that he used all five methods when he dealt with conflict. In the heat of battle with the Pharisees over his deity, Jesus withdrew (Lk. 4:14-30, Jn. 11:45-57). He used force when he drove the hucksters out of the temple (Mk. 11:11-19). During the events leading up to his arrest, trial and crucifixion he subjected himself to his enemies, as the spiritual says, "without saying a mumblin' word."

Yet he also cared deeply for people and confronted them. Remember the woman accused of adultery? He confronted her accusers with penetrating insight when he said, "If any one of you is without sin, let him be the first to throw a stone at her." To the woman he said with compassion and understanding: "Woman, where are they? Has no one condemned you?" (Jn. 8:3-11).

These two themes, love and truth, are the keys to genuine, authentic relationships. Because we cherish our marriage partner, we affirm with love and we confront with truth. We should never be satisfied with peaceful coexistence. Not even a truce will do. Our goal for marriage is mutual growth and maturity as husband and wife. Truth bathed in love best facilitates that process.

For discussion

1. *Think about recent disagreements with your spouse. What were the issues? What did you do to resolve the conflict? What are the usual outcomes?*

2. *Review the four unacceptable ways of dealing with conflict — withdrawal, smoothing over, force, compromise. Which typifies the direction of most of your conflicts? Can you think of other ways to deal with conflict?*

3. *How do you view conflict in marriage? List all of the positive results of conflict which you can think of.*

4. *Can you think of a time when you cared enough to confront in love? What were the results?*

5. *What two elements are necessary for confrontation in love? Which of these do you most need to develop? List ways in which you can develop truth and love.*

Dealing with
marital
meltdowns

11

Recently an attorney in Dallas, Tex., set a new record for severing the tie that binds. He guided forty uncontested divorces to completion in fifteen minutes. He made it look easy: a raising of the right hand, a few simple questions, a quick decree by the judge and it was all over. Forty marriages were ended. His previous record was twenty-six divorces in the same amount of time. Obviously, he was pleased with the "improvement." "I suppose it's like going to the dentist to get a tooth pulled," he said later. "There's going to be pain, but it's better to go ahead and get the pain over with and get the tooth pulled." The result of the quick divorce, he added, is "widespread happiness."

In *Divorced in America* (E.P. Dutton, 1975), Joseph Epstein paints a different picture of the divorce experience. He describes it as "an emotional ravaging that, short of starvation, imprisonment, disease and death itself, is probably equal to most that the world has to offer. . . . To go through a divorce is still . . . to go through a very private hell."

Traveling aboard a TWA 727, I was sitting next to a woman as we winged our way to the west coast. She said she was on her way to a hideaway in the mountains where she hoped to "get her head together" as she put it. She was already in her third marriage. We talked at length about the pain and hurt often caused by unhappy marriages. She observed that divorce never erases the hurt of a difficult marriage. She still felt the pain from her first marriage. She was an emotionally fractured person, the product of bitterness, hate, betrayal, rejection and guilt.

Marriages never start that way. They begin with hopes and dreams of marital success. Recently our local newspaper quoted one fellow, as he prepared for wife number *thirty-six,* as saying, "This time it's love. You can be married many times, but there's only one real love in your life." Most people feel that way.

But divorce rates continue to soar. One person described it as the "tragic melt-down" of our nuclear age. The National Center for Health indicated that in 1979 1,181,000 couples went through the melt-down, up 4.5 percent over the previous year. Divorce is not the experience of only non-Christians. It is a growing problem for Christians as well. What is an appropriate Christian response to the problem?

The divine ideal

The divine ideal for marriage is clearly present in Scripture. God's goal for marriage is the lifelong partnership of husband and wife. For men, it's a one-woman relationship for life; for women, it's a one-man relationship for life. God's ideal is fidelity and permanence in the marriage covenant. Man is to leave his parents and be *united* with his wife and "what God has joined together, let man not separate" (Mt 19:6).

Paul compares this marriage relationship with the great marriage of Christ and the church in Ephesians 5:21-33. He characterizes this relationship as mutual subjection: "Submit to one another out of reverence for Christ." This mutual subjection is then described specifically. Women are to be subject to their husbands as the church is subject to Christ. Husbands are to love their wives with the same spirit of sacrifice as Christ loved the church and gave his life for its cleansing and purification. That's the model for marriage. What a dramatic change we would see in our society if that model were lived out in every marriage.

What about divorce?

While the Bible promotes the divine ideal of faithfulness and permanence in marriage covenants, it does not gloss over the reality that marriages can end in divorce. Marital failure is an issue of concern for both the Old and New Testaments.

Two ideas surface in the biblical record concerning marital failure.

The marriage relationship can be disrupted.

Scripture suggests that marriage covenants can be broken by the sins of fornication and adultery. In Matthew 5:32 and 19:9 our Lord indicates that "anyone who divorces his wife, except for marital unfaithfulness, causes her to commit adultery. . . ." The marital relationship, therefore, is disrupted when there is sexual unfaithfulness.

Marriage can also be disrupted when one permanently leaves his or her spouse. Paul says, "But if the unbeliever leaves, let him do so. A believing man or woman is not bound in such circumstances" (1 Cor. 7:15).

Yet it is interesting that in each case divorce is not commanded, nor is it automatic. The ideal is that even in such cases the faithful partner should not break the marriage relationship but wait and work for possible reconciliation (1 Cor. 7:11). We don't just walk away from marriage when the relationship becomes difficult. Even if a Christian has an unbelieving spouse, divorce is to be avoided when possible. The goal for the believer is the preservation of the marriage.

Divorce is an admission of human failure.

The word "divorce" in the Bible means to "cut off" or to break the relationship of two people who are meant to be one flesh. Malachi, the Old Testament prophet, reminds Israel that God views the broken covenant of marriage in the same way he views broken covenants Israel made with God (Mal. 2:10-17). In the New Testament our Lord interpreted divorce as a concession of Moses for the hardness of the people's hearts (Mt.

19:8). Divorce is symbolic of the failure of two people to live together meaningfully, harmoniously and faithfully.

What about remarriage?

But when marriages fail, what does one do? Is singleness then required? Is remarriage ever permitted? In this instance Scripture is not entirely clear. G. W. Peters, in *Divorce and Remarriage* (Moody Press, 1970), suggests that this should not surprise us since the Bible never commands or legislates subideal behavior. Instead, it forbids and judges such life. The Bible encourages people who have sinned and experienced failure to turn from that life and experience the healing power of God. Since there is no clear command given for remarriage, the conclusion is implied rather than clearly defined.

There is little unanimity on the subject of the remarriage of divorced people even among scholars. The issue is controversial and no matter what one may say on the question, very reliable, competent and equally sincere people will disagree. Furthermore, judgments on the remarriage of divorced people are to a large degree a matter of human interpretation even as Paul conceded in 1 Corinthians 7:10. Still, the subject demands to be addressed, if humbly and somewhat tentatively.

Generally the following are cases where Scripture seems to free divorced persons to remarry.

For sexual immorality and refusal to repent.

Identifying the "guilty party" in an instance of sexual immorality is often a subjective thing. There are, in fact, various interpretations of Christ's words in Matthew 19:9. The clause "except for immoralities" has fueled many debates. The passage, however, seems to imply both the option for divorce in the case of the immorality of one of the partners, and the freedom for the faithful partner to remarry when the guilty party refuses to repent and live faithfully with his marriage partner. The decision to remarry, however, should not be made in haste, nor is remarriage automatically assumed. Too often couples search for excuses to abandon the relationship rather than ways to make the marriage work.

For willful and permanent desertion.

Paul suggests in 1 Corinthians 7 that the unbelieving partner is free to leave the marriage. Paul is not talking here of a hasty decision to leave, only to return a short while later. He has in mind a partner who leaves permanently and refuses to return. In such a case the marriage is over and the believing spouse, it seems, is free to remarry.

Marriage — a community matter.

It is clear from Scripture that the making and breaking of marriage covenants is no simple matter. For the Christian the marriage covenant is both a personal matter and a community matter. It is made by two people, but it is made in the company of family and friends, and within the body of Christ. Consequently, any decision to sever the relationship or to pursue remarriage is also a personal matter *and a community matter.* Marriage is never "nobody's business but my own." Members of the body of Christ are to be accountable to and for each other. Commitments made in the presence of God, one's family, friends and the body of Christ should be treated with sacred care. Any decision to break the covenant or to remarry should be made only upon the wise and prayerful counsel of the spiritual leaders of the church, and with trusted family members and friends. The role of the community of believers should be an active one, offering both healing and guidance.

It is clear from Scripture that divorce must be recognized and confessed for what it is — sin. But there is good news: divorce can be forgiven. We must continually remind ourselves that the rule of the church is grace, not law. While divorce is a tragic example of broken human relationships, it is not the unpardonable sin. Furthermore, the gospel is a witness of God's power to heal and restore the broken areas of our lives. Our commitment to the sanctity of marriage must always be graced with forgiveness to those who experience marital failure. Our

Lord set the example in his relationship with the woman accused of adultery. He said, "If any one of you is without sin, let him be the first to throw a stone at her" (Jn. 8:7). He could have been judgmental and stoned her himself, but he did not. Instead, he released her from her sin with a word of forgiveness and sent her on her way a free person.

Marriage is a gift of God, a treasure, which we have "in jars of clay" (2 Cor. 4:7). As the fellowship of the faithful let us give highest priority to stress permanence of the marriage covenant. Let us also help strengthen those marriages which seem to falter. And, let us do a better job of preparing the next generation for strong, joyous marriages rooted in Christ.

For discussion

1. *Discuss: "God's goal for marriage is the lifelong partnership of husband and wife." Do you agree? Disagree? Why?*

2. *Are divorce and remarriage sin? Always? Sometimes? Never? If divorce and remarriage are not always a sin, under what circumstances might they be acceptable?*

3. *Discuss: "Pastors should never suggest divorce regardless of how hopeless the situation." Do you agree? Disagree? Are some marriage situations hopeless?*

4. *What would you do if your marriage was falling apart? To whom would you turn for counsel and help?*

5. *What are you doing now to strengthen your marriage?*

6. *What are your attitudes toward divorced people? What is the attitude of the church toward divorced people? What should it be?*

Preventing
marital erosion

12

"Marriages are not wrecked by a blowout, but by a slow leak." These words by marriage specialist J. Allan Peterson reflect an unfortunate reality. Marriage begins with throbbing hopes for happiness and success. Too often it limps along with barely enough life to register a pulse reading.

How is it possible for tender meaningful love to turn into hurt, bitterness and anger? How is it that pleasurable physical intimacy can change into revulsion at the thought of physical contact? How can transparency, openness and honesty evolve into misunderstanding, deception and pretense?

How? Why? Unfortunately, slow imperceptible leaks can, over a period of time, flatten and ruin the best of relationships. Leaks start quite innocently, but if left unchecked they can do irreparable damage.

The husband comes home and there on the coffee table is a heap of newspapers and magazines. "Of all things," he thinks. "Can't she keep this place clean?" He mentions nothing of his irritation. Instead he embraces his wife and expresses his love to her in endearing ways.

Day two. The mess is still there. Again he ignores the irritation, embraces his wife, and gives her a light peck on the cheek.

Day three. Same story. This time angered, he cleans up the mess himself without a word to his wife. The next week the cycle begins again. Rather than dealing with his irritation, he keeps it to himself and conceals his hostility by refusing to talk about it.

One source of irritation may not amount to much, but enough of them over a period of weeks, months or years can result in permanent loss. A drip can become a rivulet; a rivulet can become a stream; a stream, a creek; a creek, a raging river. Few marriages would experience such erosion if half the sentiment expressed during courtship would continue after marriage.

How can one prevent marital erosion?

By exercising regular care and attention.

In many ways maintaining a marriage is like caring for a car. In order for a car to operate at peak efficiency it needs regular, systematic maintenance. The oil needs to be checked and changed regularly. Tires need to be inflated to the proper levels. The electrical, carburetion and cooling systems must be checked, tuned and cleaned. Ignore the need for some small repair work and major problems result. One oil advertiser puts it this way: "You can pay me now, or you can pay me later." Ignore the care and attention of one's marriage, and major problems will soon develop.

By spending time together.

There is no substitute for being together. Before marriage, each partner makes time for the other. They entertain each other and enjoy various forms of recreation together. Sightseeing, walks, attending concerts or athletic events, enjoying a good book or record is a regular part of the relationship. After marriage, though, the relationship often becomes humdrum and drab. Partners take each other for granted and often go their separate ways.

Time together doesn't just happen. It must be planned and scheduled into the week like other important parts of our lives.

By practicing active love.

What often starts with high levels of courtesy, kindness,

concern and love often winds down to a limping spirit of dull-
ness and irritability. Care and affection must be practiced, not
just longed for. The neglect of loving words and deeds begins to
crumble a relationship. "I love you" "Can I help you?" "Would
you like to talk about it?" "Let's take a walk" are loving, caring
invitations to deepen the relationship. Gifts, love letters, good-
byes, welcomes, hugs, kisses are tangible expressions of
mutual love. If a marriage is to grow, a husband and wife will
need to practice giving love-gifts to each other.

Care and affection can also be demonstrated in one's appearance. Often marriage partners who take every effort to ap-
pear at their very best during courtship become careless in
dress and physical appearance in marriage. Making oneself
physically attractive can be a gift of love to one's spouse.

By talking together.

In courtship we learn about each other through conversation. That practice should continue into marriage. Communication should include more than routine conversations about
paying the bills or concerns about children and jobs. While
such topics are important, couples also need to share their
dreams, hopes and aspirations, as well as their fears, frustra-
tions and disappointments. Silence is a sure sign of difficulty.
Inability to talk is a clue that some changes need to be made in
the communication system.

By maintaining the marriage covenant.

Covenants are unconditional agreements we make with
each other in which we promise to be faithful and responsible
to each other as husband and wife. It is surprising how casual
lovers can be about this commitment.

A couple recently came for marriage counseling. It soon
became clear that the commitment to marriage was fragile —
they were treating the marriage covenant casually. When they
were apart from each other they really didn't think of themselves as married. I suggested that to be separated during the
week by fifty or one thousand miles didn't change the marriage

covenant. They were still husband and wife. During the next session the wife was anxious to share with me how that comment had revolutionized her thinking about her marriage. She then turned to her husband and said, "Honey, I want you to know that even when I'm angry and yelling at you that I'm still your wife. That will never change." That kind of covenant will weather all kinds of marital storms.

By practicing confession and forgiveness.

It's tough to do, but it's necessary to say, "I was wrong. I am sorry. Will you forgive me?" Emotional and relational health is dependent upon our attitudes toward blame. Am I willing to assume blame when it is mine to assume, or do I pass the buck?

John Robert Clark, in his book *The Importance of Being Imperfect* (D. McKay, 1961), suggests that we need to acknowledge that we are imperfect human beings. As long as we talk and act like perfectionists we will continue to be poor communicators. Learning to communicate as imperfectionists encourages growth in relationships. Clark speaks spiritual truth. Confession and forgiveness opens the relationship to the potential for growth. The Apostle John places confession and forgiveness within the context of those qualities which foster fellowship: light as opposed to darkness; honesty as opposed to deceit (1 Jn. 1:5-9). Confession and forgiveness are basic to a strong marriage relationship.

Unfortunately, we deal with confession and forgiveness superficially. "If I was wrong . . ." is holding back the truth. "I won't hold it against him" is not sufficient. "It's okay, just forget about it" treats the issue too lightly. Individuals interested in free, open relationships are not interested in easy solutions, or in placing blame. Rather, they cherish the relationship and speak to one another firmly, clearly and freely: "I love you. You are forgiven." Furthermore, we may not be able to totally forget the past, but we can still forgive and live lovingly, caringly, freely with our spouse no matter how grievous the problem. Confession and forgiveness are those decisive acts of the will which draw the poison from the wounds that infect our memories. When the poison is gone, the wound will heal, the sensitivity will disappear, and the relationship will be strengthened.

By experiencing supernatural love.

The Apostle Paul reminds us that "God has poured out his love into our hearts by the Holy Spirit, whom he has given us" (Rom. 5:5). The love which produces strong marriages is not something we generate; it comes from outside us. It starts with God's love. Whether we received Christ long ago or just today, we have access to his love. *He* enables us to love.

Troubled marriages need the love of God. Husbands and wives may still face the same problems, but God's love can enable them to respond differently to each other. This love enables married partners to love and become lovable.

It has been said that any fool can fall in love, but to stay in love is another matter. One of the great illusions of our time is that love is self-sustaining. It is not. A relationship of love must be fed, nurtured and constantly renewed. When married people tell me that their love has died, it might be more accurate to say that their love has been asphyxiated. The suffocation of their love didn't happen by a violent, brutal act, but from sheer neglect. We take time to work and time to play, time to eat and time to sleep, time for personal interests and time for social responsibilities. Surely we can also take time to stay in love.

For discussion

1. Remember your courting days? Are you and your spouse still courting? What can you do to bring courtship romance to your marriage?

2. Think back over the seven ways to prevent marital erosion. Note specific suggestions.

a. What kind of care and attention do I need to give to our marriage?

b. *What can my spouse and I do in the next week to spend time together?*

c. *How do I need to practice active love?*

d. *What inner feelings do I need to talk about with my spouse?*

e. *How do I maintain my marriage covenant during marital storms?*

f. *Do I freely confess my wrongs to my spouse and forgive my spouse?*

g. *In what specific ways do I allow God's love to flow into me so that it may flow to my spouse?*

3. *What kind of preventative maintenance do you use to keep your marriage strong and vital?*

Growing older, growing better

13

Maybe you've seen the television commercial that shows a husband whispering tenderly in his wife's ear: "Honey, you're not getting older, you're getting better." What a compliment! It is rare for a couple to pass through the stages of courtship, marriage and parenting, come to the empty nest stage and still have a deep love and admiration for each other.

For too many people the opposite is true. J. Allan Peterson suggests that marriage is like buying a record album for just one song. We find out about the other songs on the disc when we get home. Sometimes we are pleasantly surprised; at other times we may even regret we bought the record at all. We often hope that, with time, we can at least learn to enjoy the unfamiliar tunes. As one wife confessed to me, "I knew we had some problems when we got married, but I thought we could work those out." There is always such hope.

Both people in a marriage relationship bring their unique habits and attitudes, beliefs and convictions, ways of thinking and feeling. These differences carry the potential for conflict. In addition, the various stages of marriage (founding the family, child bearing, child rearing, child launching, the empty nest and retirement) offer new challenges and opportunities for the couple. Many couples never realize when they begin their marital journey that a bundle of joy can become the focus of conflict. A couple recently observed that their son, born after ten months of marriage, had been a constant source of conflict throughout their twelve years of marriage. Many people today cynically conclude that marital bliss is nothing more than a fanciful mirage, and resign themselves to a joyless cohabitation.

Marriage can be more than an endurance test, more than peaceful coexistence, more than cohabitation. It can be meaningful and fulfilling for both husband and wife throughout the different phases of the marriage cycle. Marriages can grow richer even as the husband and wife grow older. Together they can grow to experience rich marital fulfillment.

A variety of reasons are offered in our divorce courts for marital failure, among them unfaithfulness, mental cruelty, physical abuse and incompatibility. The real reason, however, is personal failure. *Marriages fail because the people who make up marriages fail.* Generally speaking marriages disintegrate not because people marry the wrong person, or do the wrong things, but because marriage partners fail to grow and mature as individuals. Growing older and better describes a person capable of change. Growing older and better emphasizes a maturation process that begins early and continues throughout one's life.

Because of what we are

Husbands and wives desire quality in their marriages, but they usually define that quality in terms of what they do or do not do. Scripture, however, defines quality of life in terms of "being" — what one *is* and what one *can become* as a person.

In Ephesians 5:22-33 Paul presents one of the most complete of all the biblical teachings on Christian marriage. We generally read this passage in terms of what a wife is to do, and what a husband is to do if marriage is to be "Christian." We think of these twelve verses as a kind of prescription for marital success. If, however, one studies this passage in the context of the entire book of Ephesians, we learn that what we are as followers of Christ enables us to live uniquely as husbands and wives.

In the first three chapters of Ephesians Paul describes what Christians are to be. The last three chapters, including the passage on marriage, describe what believers are to do and how they are to live. The pattern is clear: what we *are to be* precedes what we *are to do*.

What are we to be as Christians? First, Paul describes our relationship to God. We are "chosen" (1:4); "adopted" (1:5); "redeemed" (1:7); "forgiven" (1:7); "made alive" (2:5); "raised up with Christ" (2:6); "saved" (2:8); "God's workmanship" (2:10); "joined together" (2:21); "a dwelling in which God lives by his spirit" (2:22). In addition, our relationship with other believers is described as being "members together of one body, and sharers together in the promise in Christ Jesus" (3:6).

This is our nature as believers. We are chosen, adopted, redeemed, forgiven.

Believing husbands and wives are also fellow citizens with the saints; fellow heirs to the spiritual kingdom; a holy temple in the Lord; the dwelling of God in the Spirit. Such a mutual relationship in Christ in the church should give us a new appreciation for the person we married. It provides for us a new conception of our uniqueness as a couple. We are both in covenant with God and with each other. We are his workmanship in Christ as two individuals and as a couple. We are the dwelling place of God as individuals and as husband and wife.

Because of what we do

In addition, Paul describes the way we are to live with each other as a walk.

We are to walk worthy of our calling as Christians (4:1-16). He describes this walk as humble, gentle, patient, forbearing, unified. He also tells us how we can enable others to grow and mature spiritually (4:12-16).

We are to walk as new persons (4:17-32). The old life is to be laid aside for the new life. Old habits, attitudes and speech patterns are to be exchanged for right and holy living, a kind and tender attitude; and a forgiving spirit.